GRANDDAD,

DID YOU WASH YOUR HANDS?

Nancy:
 Being a masochist it was really
fun being abused by Bucky and You.

Brad: She's not going to change. She
 is what she is!

 Enjoy the Great Northwest!

iUniverse, Inc.
New York   Bloomington

Granddad, Did You Wash Your Hands?

iUniverse books may be ordered through booksellers or by contacting:

iUniverse
1663 Liberty Drive
Bloomington, IN 47403
www.iuniverse.com
1-800-Authors (1-800-288-4677)

Because of the dynamic nature of the Internet, any Web addresses or links contained in this book may have changed since publication and may no longer be valid. The views expressed in this work are solely those of the author and do not necessarily reflect the views of the publisher, and the publisher hereby disclaims any responsibility for them.

ISBN: 978-1-4401-3683-2 (pbk)
ISBN: 978-1-4401-3684-9 (ebk)

Printed in the United States of America

iUniverse rev. date: 10/1/2009

TO:

HAYDEN, SETH, TREVOR, AND ELLE

Contents

PREFACE

At my wife's urging, I joined a seniors' writing class in 2001. Marynelle and I were newly married, and I had moved to her hometown of Lincoln, Nebraska. I agreed to go to the writing class if she would read my papers beforehand. I was apprehensive about sharing my writing with a body of experienced authors. But the group proved welcoming and in retrospect probably not as critical as I deserved.

I've been asked what my writing goal was at the time. It was simply to see if some of the story concepts in my head would play well in the written word. I had no objective beyond class acceptance. Every month or two for several years I wrote an essay or vignette. All were subjected to a class review. Occasionally, there were comments by some that an essay should be sent to some magazine or publication. They were never sent due to laziness or a feeling of unworthiness.

Now, after eight years meeting with the writers, I have decided to put thirty-two essays between two covers and toss it out there. Some parodies contain a bit of exaggeration that challenge the non-fiction definition, but for the most part the definition stands. The writings are of boyhood experiences, my grandchildren's humorous quotes, my wife's collectibles, genealogical searches, and of individuals, both worthy and unworthy of note.

Dinger was written (in my head) while driving to class one day. I was able to focus despite its irritating noise. *When The Iron Age Came to 5939* was a big part of my life for a couple of years. I felt compelled to share that little adventure with others. Those are examples of stories written as they occurred. I tend to reminisce with the best about long ago events. Several are included: the search by two boys for water in which to play, the general store in the nearby village, and basketball's role in rural Ohio after World War II. *Bob Eisele* has been with me for nearly a lifetime and I had promised myself to write about this man one day. The day has arrived.

In 2002 Marynelle and I stood on the slope of a Utah mountain as

1

my nephew's bobsled whizzed by. His dream of winning an Olympic medal became our dream. This exciting experience demanded telling.

One's genealogy can be excruciatingly boring to others. I risk that by including three essays. The breakthroughs I had with DNA and the research of others eliminated dead-ends of over thirty years. Hopefully, there will be those that will find it interesting and even helpful. Finding my ancestor mentioned in Thomas Jefferson's notes was a thrill. An equal thrill occurred when finding my ancestors' Virginia land was sold to the fifth president of the United States, James Monroe. Everyone should have a character like Thomas Shelton in his or her family tree.

The reader should not look for an overall theme threading through the book's episodes. Possibly, there would be one if the original plan was to write a book, but there was no such plan. The idea for a book came much later, and it was in answer to the question of what was the preferred vehicle for getting these essays "out there."

I chose to place the essays in the order in which they were written. I once read an enjoyable book by a reporter, which consisted of his newspaper columns, chronologically arranged, covering a variety of topics. I liked the lack of repetitiveness in topics, the episodic nature of the book. "*Granddad, Did You Wash Your Hands?*" is organized in a similar format.

Having made these decisions, Granddad is washing his hands of it!

DINGER

There it went again! That irritating, unrelenting sound was bouncing around within my skull. It was a difficult noise to describe to others. One had to hear it first hand. If its intent was to mimic a tiny bell, it failed miserably. It wasn't quite as metallic as a buzzer, but it was most certainly not a chime. It was a noise created by a piece of electronic gear buried in the innards of my van. Looking neither left nor right as I drove us away from the house, I squirmed awaiting her unfailing comment. "Are you ever going to get that fixed?" she asked.

"Probably, maybe someday," I replied, hoping the subject would change into something less controversial.

She pressed on, "Doesn't it bother you?"

"It bothers me more when thinking about what it'll cost to fix," I said, hoping the threat to the family budget would influence a change in topic..

Although we couldn't adequately describe the sound, we had no trouble giving it a name. We called it "Dinger", usually preceded by a descriptive adjective. The van was a year old when Dinger first arrived on the scene. I was determined to isolate and correct the problem. My efforts proved useless; there were no warning lights on the dash, all seat belts were fastened and the doors shut tight. It always happened when first starting the vehicle. However, for reasons unknown, Dinger would take a sabbatical. It would be a no-show for several days causing hopes to soar. Finally, it was gone and the ride would be quiet. But then it would return. I imagined that it must have moved to another vehicle for a change of scenery, but it came back because I still had some semblance of sanity. Its mission was not complete.

Marynelle and I were in the early phases of wedded bliss, and the "bliss" was under attack by an electronic gadget. I had to act. I kept a log: was it more active in cold weather, damp weather, windy weather, night, or was it day? The log was to give the mechanic some idea of where to start, but somehow Dinger knew when a mechanic was about to wield a wrench. At that time it would refuse to act up. With no evidence, the mechanic refused to prosecute. I could see doubt and, yes, even pity in his eyes as he would figuratively pat me on the head and send me away. I was being defeated by an electronic gizmo.

I learned to live with Dinger and Marynelle began to accept it reluctantly. The one thing consistent about Dinger was that when it did appear, it would always persist for four minutes. If you could hang on for those four minutes it would without fail, become quiet. Being resourceful and a player of games, I decided Dinger could be used as a timer. How far could I drive before it shut down? Dinger now had a purpose!

I would zip up Trelawney and out on Old Cheney. Could I get through the light at 27th and maybe 40th and beyond? There were rules: always courteous driving and keep an eye peeled for a speed gun. One day I made it through the light at 40th before Dinger shut down. I wanted to put a little mark on the curb at that very spot for future reference. I began to think of the *Guinness World Book of Records*.

Despite the new game, there was a weak moment when I returned to the repair shop. It would cost two hundred fifty dollars for something called a controller. If you drive automobiles long enough, you know intuitively when something can be repaired with little trouble. It may cost an arm and a leg, but you know it can be repaired. At the same time you know intuitively that there are malfunctions beyond the expertise of those people back there among the grease racks. I could never shake the latter feeling about Dinger. At the garage that evening I picked up the van, turned the key in the ignition, and heard the soft purring of the engine. It was a quiet ride home. Only the radio competed with the engine's hum. I drove west into a beautiful sunset. The new controller was money well spent!

The next day, we loaded the van with luggage for a weekend in Iowa. We left the driveway and headed onto Trelawney when there was an irritating, unrelenting noise. Dinger had returned! We exchanged glances and grinned, as we roared out on Old Cheney determined to get through the light at 40th and into *Guinness*.

December 2001

THE GOLD TOOTH

Dad was a small man, weighed around one hundred and thirty pounds, five feet five inches in height. He was what I would call dapper in his dress. Now, in some circles he may not have been thought dapper; but in our community he assuredly was. He was always neat in appearance, whether wearing a suit, sport coat, or sweater. As a young boy I was always proud to be seen with him.

Dad may have been somewhat vain, because he would spend more time than I thought necessary combing his hair. His finger nails were always clean and trimmed. When "dressed up," only his large hands and thick fingers were clues that he had done manual labor most of his life. He had farmed until nearly 40 years old, then worked with what he called, "machinery." As best as I could determine his real love was mechanical things although I never saw him overhaul an internal combustion engine. His one time working in an office was short lived. Right before World War II, we moved to a smaller farm in Marion County. There, he had a "desk" job at the Marion Power Shovel Company. However, he soon left the desk and moved out into the manufacturing area with the "machinery."

Dad's teeth gave him quite a challenge in maintaining his appearance. While I was growing up, he visited the dentist in LaRue often. He had fillings, bridgework where the original ivory was no more, and one false upper front tooth anchored to something I didn't understand. It seemed Dad and "Doc" Thuma had a mutual pact to beat Mother Nature. This much attention to teeth was not typical in our community. There were a lot of dentures in neighbors and among our extended family. People took the easy way out, and possibly the most economical way, by having everything pulled. And there were several around who had great gaps in their mouths, interrupted by an occasional tooth. They just let them fall out. Dad was determined not to join them.

Dad came home one night after having "Doc" ply his trade on the upper front tooth. He walked into the kitchen and smiled at us. Mom let out a gasp. A gold tooth had taken the place of where a more natural appearing tooth had been. In some cultures a lot of gold in one's mouth may be a sign of prosperity. Mom wasn't buying that. She berated the "Doc" for doing such a thing and Dad for letting him. I could tell that Dad was unsure about the tooth and had undoubtedly agreed to it in a weak moment. Our family was not in the best of economic straits; dental work was a luxury, so returning to LaRue and "Doc" Thuma was out of the question. The gold tooth stayed.

Ferne Shelton Sharp and Howard Sharp

Being young, I didn't think about Dad's visits to the dentist and what it might entail. He never mentioned any discomfort, but I was well aware of the myths surrounding dental pain and anguish. My first and only visit to "Doc" was just before entering college. I wasn't in pain but needed a dental checkup before entering Ohio University. "Doc" Thuma's office was in his home. His dental equipment looked like something out of the era before electricity, but had been rigged up to the current when the power lines came through. The solitary dental chair sat in the middle of a room that at one time must have been the parlor. The electric chair at the state penitentiary came to mind when I saw it. The equipment around the chair, some of which I couldn't identify, added to my fears. There were arms with pulleys on which were braided rubber bands to drive the drill. I was scared! The place looked archaic, even dungeon-like. I knew then the Spanish Inquisition was alive and well in LaRue, Ohio. The doctor was as humorless as his torture chamber.

I had seven fillings that day without any painkiller. Back then I'm not sure an anesthesia other than ether existed. Some of the seven fillings were only on the surface and of little consequence. But one filling in a wisdom tooth was a life-changing experience. I gripped the arms of the chair while sweat poured off me. The drill made a terrible sound, there was an odor I hadn't previously experienced, and the pain was three notches above my threshold for tolerance. "Doc" seemed irritated that I was there.

On the way home I could tell Dad felt sorry for me; but typically for him, nothing was said. He did smile though when I asked in which concentration camp he thought the good doctor had gotten his training.

After the gold tooth had been in our family for nearly a year, Dad and I were chasing some pigs that had escaped their pen. Chasing livestock was a common event on our farm because the fences were uncommonly bad. This chase was at nightfall, dark enough that only shapes could be seen. We were circling the outside of the barn, I on the west end and Dad at full speed going around the east end. I heard a thump, the sound of air taking leave of a body and after a moment some swearing. Dad had run into a post he had forgotten was there. It was a post no longer supporting anything, yet immovable when struck by a speeding human torso.

I helped Dad to his feet, and he limped to the house to check the damage. Mom, my brother John and sister Carole were in the kitchen as we entered. Dad's face had a bruise on it, but there was more. He opened his mouth and smiled at Mom. The collision had knocked out the gold tooth!

We returned to the barnyard with a kerosene lantern in search of the gold nugget. After several minutes it was spotted. Dad made an appointment with "Doc" Thuma. Whatever pact Dad and "Doc" may have had before, they were smart enough to follow some new explicit instructions from Mom. A tooth matching its neighbor was put in place. Dad's smile was back!

February 2002

TREVOR'S ARRIVAL

Oh! That was the Middletown exit I just passed! I suddenly became aware of my surroundings. I had been driving for 35 miles on a familiar interstate and could remember none of the trip. Landmarks normally seen went unnoticed. I had been deep in thought since David called. It was a mosaic of thoughts: some of the present, some of what was to be, and some of what had been. There was a seam of sadness threading through the background of all my reverie. I had been on autopilot. I needed to focus on my driving the next 25 miles to Cincinnati and David's.

Trevor Sharp and Granddad

David had said he didn't need me to come when Julia went to the hospital. Rather, he would call when the baby came. He called at 1:00 a.m. I asked the usual questions: "Is the baby okay?" which really meant, but you couldn't say it, "Were all the parts there?" I prayed a "thank you" to his positive response "Is Julia okay?" was next. "She's fine, she did great," he said and again my prayed thanks. "And the name is Trevor Ross Sharp?" I asked. "Yes," he said.

During the times we were together, before the baby came, names had been a topic. I would talk about the long tradition of continuing names in the Sharp family and thought "Ned" might be appropriate for a boy. There was no such tradition, they knew this, and would tease me about my name. *Far Side* was a popular off the wall comic page item then; and the cartoonist seemed to use the name Ned for his weirdest characters. *Far Side* cards, with Ned featured, were what I would receive from David on my birthdays. I would laugh when receiving them.

Pat had been gone a year. Wife, mother, and who would have been a wonderful, loving grandmother had lost the battle to leukemia. The "who would have been" sadness permeated our very beings. David, Jill, and I were at some level of grieving. They missed their mother and everything she was. We didn't discuss it and sensing how they were coping wasn't easy. They were both in the early phases of marriage. I hoped each of them was able to gain solace from their spouses, Julia and Dave. When we were together we could laugh and tease as before, but the loss we felt was always within reach. They were concerned about me, and I, them.

In my daily life I played a lot of "What would Pat do?" Simple household tasks might generate such a query. Mostly, though, I relied on a response to that query in my interactions with the kids. I thought about what their mother would do or expect. In my bumbling ineptness I tried to do as she would have. I hated that they had lost their mother. I was determined to be there for them in any way needed. Smothering was not my way. However, being available and having them know it, was important. In retrospect, it was important for my well-being.

Was too much expected of this baby? I looked forward to new life in the family. Would some of the sadness be erased? Is it wrong to want so much, to put so much pressure on an unsuspecting new one? Obviously, his parents were excited, but Jill and I shared in the excitement. We looked forward to the baby's arrival. Jill was great with children. Little ones seemed to gravitate towards her, and she them.

What a wonderful aunt awaited Trevor! David was a father at 30, the same age I was when he arrived in 1963. He would be a good father.

David was waiting for me when I arrived. He looked tired and somewhat relieved. His eyes were red confirming that our thoughts had been the same over the past few hours. We headed for the hospital conversing about the birth, Julia, and the baby. Julia was in Good Samaritan a few miles away.

When we entered the hospital room Julia was lying in bed with Trevor in her arms. She absolutely glowed, there was no other way to describe it. She immediately handed Trevor to me. Was I this thrilled when I became a father? Was there any facial feature that might give a hint of Pat? Trevor slept as I held him next to me. I gave another silent prayer of thanks.

Our stay at the hospital was not long. David and I went back to my car, hugged, and said our goodbyes. The drive home was much like the one going to Cincinnati: deep-in-thought , landmarks unnoticed, and—oh, that was the Middletown exit I just passed.

May 2002

WHEN THE IRON AGE CAME TO 5939

Archeologists, paleontologists, sociologists, and probably some other "ologists" tell us the Iron Age began at different times in different places in the world. One of the earliest finds has been dated around 1200 B.C. in an isolated part of Africa. It arrived in Asia and Europe at different times. I'm untrained in any of the "ologist" disciplines, but need not be trained to know the Iron Age at our house began in the year 2001A.D.

My wife Marynelle (known as Bucky in family circles) has been into old things (she calls them antiques) for many years. Until recently, most had been made of wood. Some have an interesting family history, few are functional, and two have a beauty about them that only a mother could love. One group of boards, which she calls a chest, was supposed to have been on a covered wagon going across Nebraska on the way to Oregon. The family lore has it that the chest was discarded to lighten the load when nearing the Platte River. I have researched this myth and found it wanting. What actually happened was the chest, which the husband hated, had been "secreted" onto the wagon by his wife. He, of course, had been out front with the oxen, George and Bush, for forty-five consecutive days. At the Platte, he took his first look in the wagon to see what his wife had packed. Spying the chest, he pitched it off the wagon, not to lighten the load, but for one reason only. IT WAS UGLY! Marynelle talked her siblings out of this treasure, and it now rests against the wall in our dining room.

Soon after our wedding, my wife discovered a new collectable: IRON. The first major piece of iron entering our house was a grille or gate that was supposedly from New Orleans. She wanted it mounted on the wall. It was too heavy for the wall, so little legs had to be welded at the bottom for support. An iron product goes through ten stages in its life, from being freshly forged to the final stage as a pile of rust chips on the ground. The grille was in the eighth stage fast approaching the ninth. It was so rusty tetanus refused to reside on it.

Determining the grille's age has been difficult. Sometime before

1850 is thought to be the time of its birth. I like history and think about the grille's life. I see it on Bourbon Street covering a second-story window of a house of ill repute. I see a harlot standing behind it, scantily dressed, beckoning at some desperate man on the street below. The man has just gotten off a raft after floating down the Mississippi for thirty days with a load of hogs. The lovely lady has yet to catch a whiff of him! I particularly like this vision, and it has helped me accept the grille.

However, the grille was only the beginning. Bucky went full bore. Pieces of iron were showing up in corners and on tables. I was directed to mount a piece of a "widow's walk" over the desk. I asked her about this little jewel. She said it usually resided on the upper story of houses near the coast. The wife would pace behind it while looking out to sea for her husband's ship. Given Lincoln, Nebraska's rich history as a seaport, I saw Bucky's reasoning for hanging it on the wall next to the anchor.

Armillary

I had never heard of an armillary. I was soon to learn. There are armillaries in every room and one on the lawn. Feeling frisky one day I asked her the function of an armillary. She indicated it had no purpose other than to beautify the home. At great risk I continued with my questions by asking her who Ptolemy was. I, being internet trained, had learned he was the inventor of the device in the 2nd Century. Haughtily, she informed me that of course she knew who Ptolemy was–he had played second base for the Cubs in the 1950's.

On one of our treks to Ohio, Bucky discovered iron fences. It seems Cincinnati in the 1800's was a prominent center for manufacturing of iron fences. We toured antique stores in Springfield, Waynesville, and Lebanon. In one shop she saw the fence she wanted. We negotiated for some time but found shipping costs prohibitive causing us to seek other options.

Bucky was not to be denied. She had purchased an iron gate for which she had to create a use. We had no fence for the gate and no posts on which to suspend it. She pushed ahead. She contracted for a replica of an iron fence to be made with the understanding it had to appear old. It would only be acceptable if it were in the sixth stage of corrosive decay. The fence and gate were installed.

Marynelle (Bucky) at Iron Gate and Fence

Recently, there has been a lull in the acquiring of iron. I sense a change in her interests. Could she be moving into a new search, a different collectable? I say this because the other day she asked what I thought about pink flamingos on the front lawn. This poses me with a very real dilemma. Pink flamingos I don't mind, it's whether I should now return her Christmas gift? It's a darling little armillary for the bathroom.

September 2002

OLLIE'S STORE

The term "general store" evokes memories in those of us that are "long-in-the-tooth." This is particularly so if you grew up in a rural area, either in a small town or nearby to one. Our memories of the stores will differ based on where we lived and what the locals required to sustain life. A general store in a coal mining town in West Virginia may look considerably different from a store serving the ranchers of western Nebraska. Each will have foodstuffs, but it's the other part of the inventory that will reveal the community's needs and where it is on the map.

The general store of my memory was Ollie Longshore's in New Bloomington, Ohio. As a young boy, I don't recall anyone ever saying "Let's go to Longshores's." It was always, "Let's go to Ollie's." New Bloomington probably never exceeded three hundred people in the years I lived nearby on a farm. The big business in town was the grain elevator serviced by the New York Central. There was a beer joint, a post office, blacksmith, and later, Haberman's grocery, which hurt Ollie's business. In the early part of my youth there was an auto-repair garage on the corner where Route 95 made a turn in town to go south. It was a typical Ohio village populated by people of average means.

Let me establish something before you begin to get a picture of Ollie in your mind. Ollie was a woman burdened with a man's name. We as youth, thought this funny that she would have the same name as one of our movie favorites, "Ollie" Hardy of Laurel and Hardy fame.

It may be too generous to call Ollie's a general store. It had the appearance of being such at one time, but it had regressed to carrying a few food necessities when I was a youth. One had the feeling the store had seen better days. Certainly, this must have been true when her husband was living and they operated the store together. Ollie's was on a corner across the street from the blacksmith shop. It was a two-story, wood-sided building painted white sometime in the distant past. You entered the store by going up a couple of steps in front. There was a second entrance on the south side in the back. This entrance gave access to the back of the store and to stairs leading to the home of the I.O.O.F. and Rebekah Lodges on the second floor. The first floor was divided front to back by a wall. On the left side of the wall was the store. On the right side was a room that apparently was used for storage at one time. It appeared to have been pillaged by a small army. It was piled with boxes going every which way, some opened, some not. You could only enter the room a few feet before this wall of debris cut off your path.

There were tales among us boys about what might be buried in the storage room. For me, the room had an air of mystery. One boy, assisting Ollie, had seen a box containing a pair of women's black button shoes which were the rage around 1900. Ollie expressed surprise that they were still there. One got the feeling that Ollie, herself, did not know what was in that room. One sight that always caught my eye was a large mounted sailfish on the wall. It added somewhat to the mystery of the room because the Scioto River, south of town, only gave up carp, catfish, and sunfish. The sailfish was an alien. A boy's imagination would race with thoughts of the sailfish's origin.

There was a lone gas pump out front, the kind that resides in museums today. It had a glass container at the top into which Ollie would pump the gas. There were measurements on the glass to reflect the amount being purchased. After the amount was reached, the gas would be pumped into the car. This was long before the EPA began peering into underground storage tanks for leakage and environmental damage. One can only imagine the condition of Ollie's underground tank located near the street.

Also, out front were benches used by the men during the warm months. When the weather cooled and the birds migrated, the men's instincts would kick in as well, and they would migrate to the back of the store around the pot-bellied stove. There were many lies told there. If Dan Schmidt were there, and it was rare when he was not, he would dominate the story telling. He would precede each pronouncement with, "By Jove boy now, I'm a telling ya." This would occur every 20 to 24 seconds or when he caught his breath. Today, "By Jove boy___" is the one phrase I take away from that pot-bellied stove. Dan was a genuine small town character.

During my youth I probably frequented Ollie's more than any other family member. Because of our farm's location, shopping at Ollie's was rare. Ollie's was not on my family's normal routes. I went to school two blocks (they didn't really call them blocks in villages) from Ollie's store, rode my bike there in the warm months and played ball nearby. So I was into the store more than other family members to buy what a nickel or dime could muster.

There was one aisle when entering the store. Just off to the right was the ice cream and popsicle cooler. A favorite selection was the Isaly's Klondike ice cream bar. We kids became gamblers at an early age, for if your Klondike had a pink (strawberry) center, you would get another, free. I never did. Isaly's Dairy no longer exists, but the Klondike can still be seen in some stores. Apparently, Isaly's sold the rights to the Klondike name to some conglomerate.

Walking down the aisle to the back of the store was like being in a tunnel. On the left were glass cases sitting on top of wooden bases higher than my head, and on the right were boxes of Lord knows what, also higher than my head. The dimly lit store added to the "tunnel" effect. As you progressed down the aisle the glass cases on the left gave way to a countertop. The countertop was where the transactions took place and where the NCR cash register hung out. There was candy in jars and a round of longhorn cheese under a glass cover. At the far end of the counter was a big roll of butcher paper mounted on metal brackets which contained a blade for cutting the paper to the desired length. Cheese and meat would be wrapped in the paper and tied with string hanging from a spool mounted somehow over head. In the very back of the store was the refrigerated wooden cabinet containing meat and dairy products. Ollie's was a chipped ham, bologna, and ground beef establishment. Certainly, that meat case had never seen a filet mignon or an orange roughy.

Across from the counter was where the pot-bellied stove resided. Benches on two sides of the stove were joined at a right angle leaving an area for customers to move about. Writing this, I wish my knowledge of Ollie were greater. Was she a native of the community? Did she have family now gone? Did her husband really catch that sailfish off Key West? My perspective of her is that of a young boy, but even at that I was perceptive enough to know that Ollie rivaled Dan Schmidt as a character. She had a single greeting when a male entered the store. "Whatta ya want boy?" she would say in a somewhat rough tone of voice. This, as far as I could tell, was the greeting regardless of age. When I went into the store with Dad one day and he got the same welcome, I made sure Mom knew that Dad was "boy," too.

Candy bars, a much needed item for a boy's growth, provided an adventure when buying out of the glass case. Ollie would be told which candy bar you wanted. She would start down the back of the counter on her way to peer inside the case to pick out the Hershey bar. You would be out of sight to her, and she, to you, until she opened the back of the case, put an arm in and sometimes peered about. She had to do this because the case was a mess. Candy boxes were strewn about. What you saw from your side of the case was not always what she saw from her side. She would move the boxes about until the Hershey would reveal itself. When it was found and you had paid for it, the next test was its edibility. There were times candy purchased looked as if it had been delivered the same day as the high button shoes back in the storage room. I could never eat dark chocolate candy that had turned white with age. And I was too timid to take it back.

Doing justice to a description of Ollie, her appearance and stature, is undoubtedly risky after so many years. I didn't have an eye for woman's fashions but I knew Ollie, and her dress, missed the mark. *Vogue* would not have approved. When I picture her today I see layers of clothing. A print dress, an apron, sweater buttoned up the front, and if it were cold, a jacket of some sort. All of this was worn in the store. She had brown hosiery and black shoes with a low, wide heel. The sides of the shoes were run over to the point that they would soon be leaving the soles behind. But her real trademark was a well worn black felt hat, round crown, floppy brim all around. A hole or two would be seen in the crown. It was worn everywhere no matter the season. If New Bloomington had a museum, and it doesn't, that hat would be prominently displayed.

After Ollie's husband died, she lived at Nydia Black's, a short walk from the store. Nydia worked with Ollie at the store. They were both short, Nydia a bit more slim. Ollie was not especially wide in the beam, but you didn't share the store's aisle with her. It was not unusual to buy something; and while walking out of the store, hear Ollie ask Nydia, "Who was that boy?" As you exited would hear Nydia reply, "That was the Sharp boy."

Ollie and Nydia sort of operated like the "bad cop, good cop" do in interrogations. The bad cop comes at the suspect first, grills him hard, then leaves the room. The good cop takes over to the immense relief of the suspect, who then pours his heart out to the nice man, confessing all. Ollie was gruff, very direct, and somewhat intimidating while Nydia was more demure, talked in a softer voice, and was much less threatening to a small boy. However, they had one thing in common. They fell asleep a lot on the benches near the stove. It was not unusual to find them both sitting up, sound asleep when entering the store. I'm certain a deft thief could have cleaned them out if one chose. Actually, they could have resided undetected in the storage room for weeks while cleaning them out.

Ollie and Nydia would close up the store and go home for the night. The day's receipts went with them along the darkened street. They were never accosted, a cent never lost.

If pretentiousness was at one end of the scale, Ollie was at the other end. She was comfortable in her setting: a small town started by an ancestor, a business begun with her long deceased husband, and knowing the world through her customers' experiences. Her isolation was reinforced by her lack of mobility as she did not drive or own an auto. Ollie and the store were hand-in-hand as they neared the end.

Today, the corner lot stands empty.

January 2003

THE 2002 WINTER OLYMPICS

The hill ahead looked manageable, one I could climb under normal circumstances. But these were not normal circumstances, for I was bearing layers of clothes, wearing boots better suited for a moon-walk, and carrying a backpack with the items to survive a winter's day on a mountain. Marynelle was maintaining a pace so as not to leave me behind. We were not alone as we climbed upward, passing some, being passed by others. The Swiss were the real show-offs. They were lugging huge bells on their shoulders as they passed on either side of us. A Swiss cow laden with one of the bells around her neck would have a difficult time keeping her hind feet on the ground. Obviously, they had been cast to deafen anyone within one hundred yards, as we were to find out.

We were trudging upward to the start of the bobsled run with hopes for a good showing by the USA. My nephew, Doug Sharp, had made the USA-2 Bobsled as a pusher. We were excited, expectant, and a bit nervous for Doug and his big moment. It was the 2002 Winter Olympics in Park City, Utah.

We had decided to go to Utah if Doug's sled qualified, so all through the winter, via the internet, I watched bobsled results in the World Cup. I sent for tickets when it appeared Doug's sled would qualify. They were sold out! I went on e-bay, found tickets, made a bid, and nervously waited for several days. Ultimately, I won both the Giant Slalom and 4-Man Bobsled tickets. We were off to buy long johns.

We watched weather forecasts for several days looking for the best time to cross western Nebraska and Wyoming on our way to Utah. The weather was cold on our drive, but there were no blizzard conditions and little snow. Our overnight stop was at a motel in Evanston, a few miles from the Utah line. The next morning the weather was cold and the sky clear, a beautiful winter day in the mountains on our drive into Park City.

The Utah Olympics opened February 10th. The bobsled competition was at the end of the games, the 22nd and 23rd. We arrived Thursday, the 21st. We parked, grabbed a shuttle and headed for the downtown to size up the place and sense the atmosphere. Park City was alive with people, all seemingly happy and excited to be a part of the scene. The clothing apparel contract for the U.S. team had been given to the Roots Corporation from Canada. Their logo was prominently displayed on jackets, sweatshirts, and tams seen on the street. Soon we were in a long line in their store purchasing tams for Marynelle, my daughter Jill, and granddaughter Elle.

That afternoon we went to our first event, the Giant Slalom. Security for all the venues was tight, slowing entry as bags were searched, but the attitude of both the personnel on duty and the spectators trickling through the gates was upbeat. It was as if all understood the need for security and together they would reduce risk as much as practical. 9/11 was fresh in our memories.

We found places a short distance up the Giant Slalom course beyond the finish line. We were able to see the skiers come into view as they approached the bottom third of the run. Times were announced as they passed different points on the course, so as they came into view we knew which ones were the most competitive. After a couple of hours on the mountain, thoughts of a trip back to town and hot chocolate won the day.

Friday morning early we went to the bobsled venue, entering one of the long lines to be screened and gain entrance. There was a good deal of bantering between those in line and Olympic volunteers standing on the side. All were friendly and in a good mood. The workers would holler out, "Where are you from?" And those in line would respond with "Los Angeles," "Seattle," " Illinois," "Austria." They would be met with "Welcome" or an "Oo" or an "Ah." There was silence when we said, "Nebraska."

After climbing upward and sweating profusely under our layers, we arrived at the starting line for the bobsled. There, we met Doug's family: my brother John, his wife Sherry, my niece Kendra, and her husband Ray. There were other family members and friends along the course to cheer for Doug's sled. Kendra made sure Marynelle and I had "USA-2" painted on our cheeks.

We positioned ourselves in the stands so that we could see the teams in the "push" part of the run, see them jump onto the sled, disappear around a curve heading off for a thrill on ice. Times were announced and posted on a scoreboard at different points along the route. The "push" phase is critical for a successful competitive run. Doug's sled was being driven by Brian Shimer, a 39-year-old veteran driver in his last Olympics. He had never won a medal in previous Olympics but had been having some good runs in the World Cup. He was coming back from a serious injury.

The World Cup for bobsled is held each winter with competitions in Europe, Canada, and the U.S. The results from these events determined which sleds would represent the USA in the Olympics. It also provided the basis for the starting order for all sleds in the Olympics. Typically the early runs have some advantage since the course is in good condition and not as chopped up as it is for the later entrants. The bobsled event consists of four runs over two days. The accumulative time of the four runs determines where the competitors place.

Each country could enter two sleds. USA-1, driven by Todd Hayes, was to go down in the first group of ten entrants. Todd had been a pusher who had become a very good driver. He and his sled were ranked high in the World Cup series. The USA-2 sled was to run in the eleven through twenty group of entrants. Swiss and German teams had been the best finishers in the meets that winter and were favored in the Olympics.

The excitement built as each team stepped to the line and began preparation for the start. The cheering escalated when the German, Swiss, and USA sleds came to the line. The bell-ringing Swiss were by far the loudest and for some reason they appeared grim and less congenial than the other spectators. Possibly it was the climb with the great weights on their shoulders that contributed to their attitude.

The riders took their positions, pushed their sled back and forth while shouting and making guttural sounds, got into a rhythmic count, then charged hard across the starting line, and down the course. The driver went into the sled first, the two pushers in sequence, and finally the brakeman at the rear. The "push" is a key part of the run, the impetus for the sled's start downhill. Previously, I had thought the brakeman applied brakes as necessary during the run. However,

I learned the sled is essentially in freefall to the finish steered by the driver along the best line to maximize speed. Riders can experience 4 G-forces in the big curves. The brakes come into play after the sled crosses the finish line.

USA-2's First Run

A scoreboard at the start kept everyone apprised of the progress down the run by posting times at different points down the track. When USA-1 and USA-2 came up we, among many, were in full throat cheering them off. We followed their progress, our eyes riveted to the board. The "start" times were announced immediately then we would wait almost breathlessly for the next time check, and the next, until the run was completed.

After all entrants had run that morning, USA-1 was in the top ten group which was important for positioning in the next run coming up. USA-2 was near the top of the second group of ten, not in a good position to place high. They were three tenths of a second away from those in "medal" position, a very deep hole to overcome in a sport measured in hundredths of a second. Brian Shimer, the driver of Doug's sled, had missed third place in the 1998 Nagano Olympics by two one-hundredths of a second. Once again it appeared Shimer would miss out on a medal.

Saturday dawned another beautiful day in the Wasatch Mountains. There was a bit of wind during the day's runs. We stood midway down the course by the tightest and longest curve on the track. It must have been nearly 180 degrees for we could face the curve, turn completely around and see the sleds come out of the curve. They were reaching speeds of 70 to 80 miles per hour. Despite the mere hundreds of a second separating the sleds, you could sense the differences in speeds as they flashed by on the curve. This was a popular viewing area where the largest group of spectators gathered. I'm sure we looked more at the teams' times and places than we did at the bobsleds zipping high in the banked curve in front of us. The scoreboard told the story.

Shimer and USA-2 had an unbelievable final day. They had the second fastest time in the morning run to move into the fifth position overall. We nervously awaited the fourth and final run. The weather had turned gray and colder. We decided to go to the finish line to watch the USA sleds come in. There, too, were bleachers and places for the spectators. We were near the track where the sleds were braking to come to a stop. I edged to the fence, leaned over and snapped a shot of Doug's sled coming in.

We knew the German-2 team had held on to win first place, but for a few minutes the outcome for the silver and bronze medals was not clear. Suddenly, the crowd erupted. USA-1 was second and USA-2 was third. They were the first bobsled medals for the USA in forty-six years! Shimer had his medal. He and his team of Doug Sharp, Mike Kohn, and Dan Steele were ecstatic!

Marynelle and I were part of the celebration, jumping up and down and yelling. I embraced my teary-eyed brother, a father proud of a son who had a dream of one day being in the Olympics. A dream now crowned with a bronze medal!

Doug and Me

There was a small stand placed at the finish to honor the medal winners. The official award ceremony would be the next day in Salt Lake City. But no delayed recognition could top the celebration already taking place. When Doug and his teammates mounted the stand each had an American flag and a bouquet of flowers. Family and friends cheered, all beamed and cameras flashed. The Swiss bells were silent.

The next day we were invited to attend a Bobsled and Skeleton Federation brunch to recognize all participants in the events which the Federation governed. The women had won gold medals in both the bobsled and the skeleton so there was much to celebrate. We met many of the athletes and Geoff Bodine, the NASCAR driver and owner. He had used his race car design and technical sources in making the USA bobsleds. It was a great experience to mingle and meet with these people.

The 1980 USA hockey victory in the Olympics at Lake Placid had inspired a young boy to one day become an Olympian. Twenty-two years later the dream was realized. During that time Doug Sharp never lost his focus, had a goal, and kept it within sight. It was tenacity in the extreme.

Now, Doug will be the inspiration for the next generation of young boys and girls.

May 2003

MELTDOWN

It was the lilt in her voice that caused a reflection,
Should I look west, change my direction?

Our memories were good, she of he, I of her,
Now both were gone, we each to endure.

We decided to meet, drawn by the past,
What the future held we dared not ask.

I saw her come in, go straight to the clerk,
Unseen, I watched her, in a bit of a lurk.

She turned to the room and began to scan,
Then there was that smile, the meltdown began.

October 2003

THE ZIPPER CLUB

I have never been a joiner. Organizations, causes, clubs, and such are carefully reviewed before I consider joining up. I have found there is usually a money and time commitment when you do join. I'm more protective of my time than money, the latter of which wouldn't float any group for long. I've never understood those people with paragraph after paragraph of organizations listed in their obituaries. How could they ever be effective if they spread their participation among so many? Did they have a personal life; did their spouse and children ever see them? When I do join, I commit, and am somewhat critical of those that serve in name only.

My philosophy on joining was recently put to a test. I was given an opportunity to join a club that would take a significant amount of time and money. I chose to join with little review or questioning; an act completely out of character for me. I joined The Zipper Club.

A few days ago it was determined I needed heart by-pass surgery. A failed stress test, a day with a heart monitor, a heart catheter all in a matter of hours resulted in the surgeon's sitting across from me reviewing my options: surgery tomorrow morning, take a few days to think it over, or do nothing. Since I have a few things that remain undone in this world I chose to join up the soonest—tomorrow morning was selected.

Those that have had this procedure are called members of The Zipper Club because of a zipper-like scar running up the chest. There was no hesitancy on my part about joining up. No questions were asked about the cost or time commitment. I desperately wanted in the club because of the supposed benefits. When Marynelle and I married, rather late in life, we pledged many years together. To have a shot at holding up my end of the bargain, an operation was in order.

The surgery was successful but my hospital stay was prolonged to implant a pacemaker to correct an erratic rhythm problem. This limits my participation in contact sports. Sumo wrestling has been ruled out.

I am now in the recovery mode. Cardiac rehab starts next week. In the interim, Marynelle's son, Todd, perks up the day with his visits. Amazingly, I'm pain-free. I have little appetite which all the medical types say is bad; you need to eat to heal. Secretly, I'm hopeful the suit I was married in will again fit. I'll try it on in a few days.

Right now, I need a nap.

December 2003

GRANDDAD, DID YOU WASH YOUR HANDS?

I just took one of my best friends in the whole world to the airport. He and his sister were visiting over New Year's. His name is Seth and he's my seven-year-old grandson. His sister Elle is three. They flew in from Ohio while their parents went on to Tempe on a four-day holiday at the Fiesta Bowl.

Seth is a wonderful little boy who shows signs of being quite big someday. He has the good looks of his parents. He tends to be rather serious and somewhat of a worrier. At the same time he can break me up with some of his pronouncements. When younger, his comments were not intended for belly laughs, but as he has gotten older a mischievous grin lets you know a tease of a seven-year-olds' riddle is on its way.

Both Dave and Jill worked, so Seth had a baby-sitter until he was old enough for daycare. At that time he went to a rather fundamentalist church with a very large kindercare, kindergarten and when Seth was six, a first grade. Seth flourished in this environment as he became a miniature version of Oral Roberts with a bit of Jerry Falwell thrown in. He would quote Bible verses and on occasion profess dire circumstances if such and such occurred.

I, of course, with my liberal attitude about religion loved this. I told his parents that I saw a future for Seth on the revival trail, traveling from town to town through the Midwest with his tent. To keep up with his Biblical knowledge I gave his mother an Interpreter's Bible for Christmas. However, I wasn't sure his church school was open to any interpretation of God's Word.

I suppose all five-year-olds see things in black or white terms. There is no gray, it is either yes or no. Seth certainly sees things that way when it comes to driving my van, all to my benefit I might add. I sometimes fasten my seat belt as I start off. Seth lets you know that the vehicle moves only after the belt is secured. One time the back of my van was crammed full, taking away his seat. We had to go about five blocks to his friend's house. He wouldn't get in the front, only in the back, so I had to move enough junk to provide him a backseat. Could that be his parents' training, the kindercare's or both?

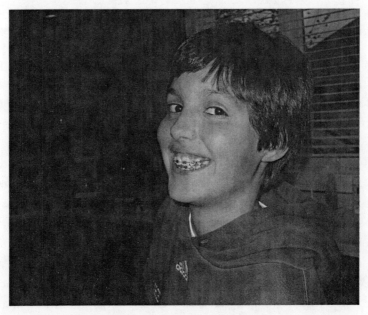

Seth Buffenbarger (older here)

Some of our fun times together have been on hikes in Glen Helen near Yellow Springs. It's a beautiful wooded area with a few virgin white oaks that escaped the ax in the 1800's. It has streams, cliffs, and some foundations remaining from the water powered industry that existed back then. On one hike we had gone about two hundred yards when Seth asked, "Granddad, how many miles have we gone?" I knew then that the hike would not be a long one.

One hike on a beautiful day was deep into the woods, almost to John Bryan State Park, which is a bit long for a five-year-old. There were deer that crossed our trail up ahead, and I thought he would be impressed. However, he was more concerned about the potential bear lurking around every tree. Before the hike was over, I was looking around every tree.

Some of his comments and actions at different ages that I found humorous are recalled with help of his mother:

. Eighteen months–Seth called the vacuum cleaner "Boo." Most of the time "Boo" was a monster that stayed in the closet when not in use. Peeking into the closet was scary and never done. Eventually, "Boo" became a friend.

Eighteen months–How exactly, no one knows, but Seth dialed 911. The operator asked if it was an emergency and he responded "yes" ("yes" and "no" were the major words in his vocabulary). The parents learned of the "emergency" when the sheriff's deputy knocked on the door.

Two-years-old–Seth, upon learning he had not been born when his parents' home was being built, asked, "Where was I?" "You were in Mommy's stomach," Jill replied. And he came back with, "Why did you eat me?"

Four-years-old–Seth, Jill and I went to the Nichols family reunion in Lafayette, Indiana. We stayed overnight in adjoining rooms at a Holiday Inn. Seth announced he wanted to sleep with Granddad. I was secretly pleased, despite the fact sleeping with him was like sleeping with a billy goat. About 3:00 a.m. I roused to take my usual bathroom visit. I quietly returned to bed, crawled in and was surprised to hear this tiny, sleepy voice,

"Granddad"

"Yes."

"Did you wash your hands?" I had not, but immediately did so, while laughing.

Four-years-old–Seth told me that I smelled like an old person.

Four-years-old–On one of our hikes the "urge" hit him. I was able to convince him it was okay to go in the woods. He learned another purpose for a tree.

Five-years-old–While fishing with me he was stung by a catfish feeler. I never appreciated the importance of Band-Aids as a cure-all until that moment. I had to drive to the nearest store to buy them before the crying stopped.

Five-years-old–On a hike one day he announced he had to "poo." Such action in the woods was unthinkable for him, so I hurriedly drove to a nearby putt-putt golf course. He decided he no longer had to go. A series of "Yes, I do," "No, I don't," took place until I drove him home to familiar surroundings. I placed him on the "john" while he continued to protest. He was directed to stay there and get the job done. After about ten minutes he announced, "Granddad, I can't go, it's stuck on my bones." Picturing this, I gave up.

So, those are some of Seth's funnies. "Out of the mouths of babes" is something we need to experience on occasion. Those little rascals provide a fresh, unvarnished look at the world.

February 2004

THE YEAR I TURNED PRO

It was in 1945, late February, the day of the finals for the County High School Basketball Tournament. Basketball was my passion then. It took several years before girls edged out basketball, and then it was only by a nose.

Our school gym had been built by the WPA in 1939. It was a beautiful structure with about 250 permanent seats, enough for the small community in which it resided. Temporary seating would be placed on the stage on the other side of the floor if the crowd were large. The floor was varnished with several coats and kept highly polished. We were never permitted to wear street shoes on that floor.

New Bloomington hosted the county basketball finals during a ten-year span. There were twelve schools in the county, all small, for this was before consolidation into fewer and larger schools. When Marion built the coliseum on the fairground, the tournament in its entirety moved there in 1950. Our gym floor was not the same size as those today, not as wide or long. However, it was the best gym in the county, certainly the newest, with the greatest potential for squeezing the crowds in that would come to the finals. There was a key consolation game for third place at 7:30 and the championship game followed. Three teams would be eligible to go on to the state tournament. Because of this, the outcome of the 7:30 game carried nearly as much interest as the one for the championship.

The gym would be packed; probably the village experienced its biggest crowds during those times. Fans would begin to line up outside the school shortly after noon on Saturday. Doors would open in the afternoon. All the permanent seating and the stage seats would be gone by 4:30, three hours before the consolation contest. People would bring food and play cards and games to while away the time. Once while in grade school I walked three miles from home to the finals on a spring-like day in February. I was stunned to see so many people there at 4:00 o'clock. I worried that Dad might not be allowed in when he finally arrived at 6:30.

The tourney was the big chance for the junior class to finance their trip to Washington, D.C. and New York City. They had the concessions where sloppy joes, hot dogs, popcorn, pie, and chili were served. The students, parents, and teachers pitched in to take advantage of this once a year "mother lode" of customers. Spectators confined for over six hours, only leaving their seats if a trusted friend or relative would save it, had to be fed and provided drinks.

Harry Alexander, our coach, decided something had to be done to break the monotony for those awaiting the 7:30 game. His solution was to schedule our 6th graders against the 6th grade team from Pleasant. We were to play at five o'clock and, hopefully, provide a little entertainment for those already packed into the gym. "Packed in" requires explanation. People were permitted to sit in all the aisles and stand against the walls up in the bleachers. People would sit and stand on the stage. Those on the stage might see one end of the floor but not the other as people pressed forward.

The "packing in" was not over. Next the custodian and helpers would put folding chairs around the entire floor back of the out-of-bound lines. Then, as fans continued to come in they would place them two deep, against the walls, behind the chairs, around the floor. When this occurred the chairs would inch onto the floor causing the black out-of-bounds lines to disappear. The lines would never appear again until the games were completed and the crowd left. Spectators' knees became out-of-bounds when the ball touched them. A player throwing the ball in-bounds had to back against someone's knees. The tilting backwards of a spectator's head when approached by a sweat-drenched player was one of the more entertaining sights during the games.

Basketball players were shorter back then. However, for a span of several years our boys were shorter than most. I was the shortest of the short. It was as if a spell had been cast on us by some terribly wicked witch pointing her wand at us saying, "You will be undersized, especially the Sharp kid." When you are short, people tend to assume you are agile and fast. The "spell caster" took care of that one as well. We had some of the slowest, short boys south of Lake Erie.

To appear in front of such a large crowd as a 6th grader was beyond our wildest dreams. I thrived on it, though there were some derisive remarks directed towards me like—"look, he most be a fourth grader" and "wow, look at his bowed legs." The crowd was on top of us and I heard it all. Early in the game I had to take the ball out. I headed to where the referee was holding it for me. I approached a pair of knees, against which to back, when a young man standing behind the chairs held out the palm of his hand, "I'll give you this money if you make a basket." I didn't know him or his woman companion, as they were not from our community.

To that point in the game I had not made a basket. Possibly the man felt his money was safe or maybe he felt sorry for the little kid. My being small was somewhat of an advantage because the other team tended to ignore me. As a result, I was free a lot, darting around making myself available for a pass. When I threw the ball in-bounds I received it back, drove to the basket and scored. I turned and pointed at the man. After the game I walked over to him and collected fifty cents.

Later, I began to worry. Did this make me a professional? I knew amateurs were not to take money for athletics. I knew Jim Thorpe's Olympic medals had been taken away because he had been paid to play football. All of us boys had heard that story. Had the 50 cents tainted my future? Would my dream of playing high school ball, like the big boys I so admired, be dashed? How many people saw the exchange of money and handshake between the man and I after the game? I regretted my impetuous act of turning and pointing to him after making the basket.

This concern was soon forgotten, for it was now spring, and baseball was in the air.

Years later, in the 1970s, we lived 80 miles from New Bloomington. The minister at our church had decided the congregation needed a spiritual recharging and a team of lay people from other churches came to do just that. Pat and I had volunteered to host one couple for two days over a weekend. We were introduced to Warren and Loretta Kramp, who were from LaRue, Ohio, a town near New Bloomington. I remember Dad talking about the Kramps, but I didn't know them since they were in a different school district. Over the weekend we reminisced about Marion County and found we knew many of the same people. Sports were a major part of the discussions. As the weekend wore on I began to sense something familiar about Loretta for she had unusual red hair. It was a shade not often seen. The man, that night I scored the basket, had a pretty young woman with him with red hair. After studying Warren closely I decided to tell him about my 6th grade experience that night at the tournament. Warren said it was Loretta and he standing behind the chairs along the sideline. It was he who had given me the fifty cents. We laughed at the coincidence of meeting after twenty-five years.

At the end of their weekend stay, I apologized for my cocky behavior that night on the basketball floor—especially the turning and pointing at him. As we bid them goodbye I slipped him fifty cents.

April 2004

BOB EISELE

Growing up in the 40's and 50's in rural Ohio, we were more attuned to seasonal events related to plant life than our city cousins. Farming and the activities supporting it were "season-dependent." The spring planting and the fall harvest were as certain as the earth's 24-hour rotation. You did not need a calendar to tell it was time to shear the sheep in the spring or make hay in June. If the harvest was good and the price of grain up, some new clothes or a new appliance might appear, but only after all the outstanding bills had been paid. The clearing of out-standing debts did not escape the influence of seasons.

Even our diseases were seasonal. Flu struck the hardest in the winter, and the dreaded polio was most virulent in the summer. Another seasonal happening, one experienced by way too many families, were farm accidents. On the farm, accidents were not relegated to a particular period in the year, but the fall harvest was when many accidents happened; sometimes the deadliest. It was almost as if the tractor and the equipment pulled and driven by it had been thrust on the farmer; a farmer ill-prepared for the negative side of mechanization. A farmer who knew horses and horse-drawn farm implements, but had now transitioned to power-take-offs, corn pickers, combines and hay balers. The horse was no longer the "tractor."

Looking back, I marvel that my father escaped serious injury. He was a man who darted about and sometimes attacked farming tasks as if he were in battle. Safety did not appear to be uppermost in his mind when he was in the "attack" mode. He did lose the ends of two fingers when setting up a new corn picker for a farmer. He was removing cornstalks that had clogged the picker, the farmer's foot slipped on the tractor's clutch, and the ends of Dad's ring and middle finger of his left hand were removed. Thankfully, no other significant harm was experienced by him in his years around machinery.

Uncle Claude, Mom's brother, barely escaped death one day while pulling a potato digger driven by the tractor's power-take-off. His clothes became entangled in the take-off's shaft. Fortunately, his bib overalls were well worn. He managed to hold on as his faded clothes were ripped from his body. Battered and bruised, covered with a few strips of denim, he walked across the field to U.S. 30 and flagged down a motorist for a trip to the hospital. I heard this story many times as a boy.

Tragedy visited so many over the years. A former schoolmate fell into a bin of shelled corn and suffocated. Two years later his wife overturned a tractor onto herself and was killed leaving several children parentless. Farm tragedies had a devastating impact on a rural, close-knit community. One either knew the victim or someone close to them.

Bob Eisele was a neighbor that farmed his 80 acres as well as our small farm of 60 acres. Bob was the antithesis of Dad, for he was deliberate, contemplative, and went about his work at a pace that suggested time was not a limiting factor in getting into the fields. He had not gone to college, but he was what Dad called "well read," which meant he was intelligent. He was president of the County Farm Bureau, a Sunday School Superintendent and considered a community leader. Although they were different, I could tell Dad had a great deal of respect for Bob, which I believe was reciprocated.

My first real job away from home was working for Bob. It started with mowing the yard (we didn't call it lawn back then) and progressed to helping with hay and grains in the summer. I was not familiar with many of the activities around the farm equipment; but I had the best instructor a young, unsure boy could have. I made mistakes, had to be shown how to do something more than once, which would have frustrated Dad, but Bob took it in stride. Bob did not use profanity. His strongest attempt at it always came out, "Oh sugar." Without a doubt, a young boy could not have had a better teacher, guide, and if I were to use today's terminology, mentor.

Bob Eisele was the most patient, kind, and sensitive man I have ever encountered. He exhibited these characteristics in everything he did. On a farm, livestock many times are abused; but he treated animals with care. He was respectful of people in his comments. Obviously, he was a great influence.

He was a bachelor in his late 30's when I worked for him. This, the neighborhood women, and not a few of the men, thought was a waste.

They saw a man who would be a wonderful husband and father. Even I agreed on the father part, being uncertain what constituted a wonderful husband. One day, the neighborhood wishes were answered when Bob married Evelyn, and in quick order there were three children: Cheryl, Charleen, and Dennis.

However, this cautious, deliberate, man fell victim to the corn picker as well. Those of us who knew Bob could not believe that he would become careless like so many before him. He lost his arm below the elbow. I learned of the accident while away in college and was able to see him in the hospital when home on a weekend. Later, back at school, I learned that he was fighting an infection. When I returned home for Thanksgiving holiday, there was a stop to drop off a friend at his home. It was there I learned that Bob had died that day.

I was devastated. I had experienced deaths of relatives: aunts, uncles, and a grandparent, all advanced in age, but this one seemed so unfair. His three pre-school children were never going to experience what I had—a caring, loving, gentle man who was meant to be a father. To this day, I lament his family's loss.

May 2004

I DID WRITE IT DOWN!

I'm forgetful–always have been, and I have no plans to change. I can be easily distracted, attention sidetracked to disparate reaches while in the midst of an ongoing activity. Missed appointments, birthdays, due dates over the years would fill a book, which demands writing, if I could just remember what was missed. Embarrassment and chagrin have followed some of my more significant foul-ups. It is at those times I resolve to get focused, and to ignore the extraneous. But the focus is short-lived. The old concentration fragments, freeing my mind to muddle through.

"Why didn't you write it down?" she implores. "I did write it down," is the retort, "but I can't remember where!" I have tried lists, writing down appointments, things that require doing, upcoming events; but the lists take on a life of their own and wander off. The first three "to-dos" might get accomplished, the remaining thirty-one actions get short shrift. It is a race between the mind and the list itself as to which will be first to go astray.

Possibly organization, or lack thereof, is an off-shoot of my forgetfulness. It is not unusual for me to have several "projects" in differing stages of completion. Projects involving paper work are scattered about my office. I have always been suspicious of managers in the work place with a clean desk top. I never had a clean desk top while working in an office. Now, retired, I carry on this practice. Sitting at my desk one can look about at "projects" in some state of being worked. They cover the desk top. And some have migrated to the floor. They consist of stacks of papers, each carefully placed so that their identities can be maintained. I have learned that one must not place different "projects" close to one another, particularly on the floor. If one does err in this regard, a chemistry seems to occur in which the papers form an attraction to each other. They will begin inching toward one another until a merger of sorts occurs. Papers intermingle, thereby resulting in a loss of their original identity and intent.

My all-time memory lapse occurred with my wife Pat. We always

Pat Sharp

had our two vehicles serviced at Jack's, a garage and service station a mile away in Enon, Ohio. One cool fall day the car required some maintenance, so we delivered it in the morning before I went to work. Pat threw on a raincoat over her pajamas and drove the car to Jack's. I followed in the van and drove up in front of the station to go in to talk to Jack himself about what needed to be done. Pat had parked off to the side where cars to be serviced resided. After talking to Jack, I jumped into the van and drove to work, forgetting my pajama-clad wife awaiting me to take her home. In the evening, after I had returned home from work, Pat asked about my day. It was a couple of hours later that she prodded my memory further by asking if I were going to apologize. I asked, "What the heck have I done now?" Then I learned what I had and hadn't done.

When I drove the van away that morning, Jack, standing inside the station saw what was happening. He looked at Pat, threw up his arms, and shrugged. Pat watched the van go down the street, saw my brake light come on, and "knew" that I was coming back. But I drove on. Jack had to take her home. Pat expected a phone call from me during the day, remembering, then apologizing. There was no call; my mind was elsewhere. It was a classic episode of forgetfulness, the kind that would cause me to self-flagellate mentally and pledge to do better.

And I did do better–I never forgot Pat at Jack's again!

July 2004

MR. DONNELLY

"What do you want to be when you grow up?" It's a question usually posed by a grandparent or a favorite uncle. If the child is young enough, the occupations tend not to vary widely. A little boy will say fireman or policeman; sometimes, little girls the same. It must be the uniforms. A child never expresses a desire to be a Shakespearian actor. That desire comes much later after accumulating a four hundred thousand dollar debt in pursuing an advanced degree in computer science.

My son, David, decided to be a garbage collector at a very early age. The garbage truck that came down our street was of extreme interest to David. When the truck could be heard stopping at each house, David would drop everything he was doing, breakfast included, rush to the couch, and stand on it to see out the front window. It was a major event.

Mr. Donnelly was the driver of the truck and owner of the business. He would wave at David, sometimes tap on the window and get a wave and a grin in return. This went on for some time. They looked forward to seeing each other those two days each week. A bond was formed. Mr. Donnelly would give David a Christmas present and card with a note written on it. On one collection day David was ill and could not go to the window. Mr. Donnelly knocked on the door to see if something was wrong.

One day, there was another knock. Mr. Donnelly wanted to know if David could ride on the truck. Pat gulped, said, "Sure," with little conviction; and off the little boy went to pick up trash and go to the dump. There was a stop at the Donnelly's home to meet Mrs. Donnelly. It was the ultimate experience for a three-year-old boy with his eye on the future as a "trash man."

When David was four we moved to a new home. It was fifteen miles away and not served by Mr. Donnelly. However, the relationship continued via notes and cards, especially at Christmas. David, in turn, would send some of his artwork to the Donnellys. On one occasion the Donnellys came to pay David a visit for which he was thrilled.

As the years passed, the cards and notes arrived at Christmas until one year Mrs. Donnelly wrote that her husband had died. The relationship did not end there for Mrs. Donnelly continued to write letters into her nineties. Ultimately, she lost her eyesight and would have a niece or grandchild write a note to this boy who had become a forty-year-old man.

> I have a soft spot in my heart for the Donnellys. Every parent wants people around their children who are good influences—warm, caring people of trust. This man, who with a little boy, managed to smear both sides of a picture window each week, was an excellent influence. David, in his first selection of a friend outside the family circle, made a fine choice. It is a good memory for a father.

> September 2004

"DO YOU WANT TO PLAY PASS?"

I catch myself watching the grandkids–looking for signs that their expressions, looks, voices, movements, and interests suggest someone who has contributed to their gene pool. I did it at their birth and continue to do so as they grow up. Admittedly, humanity would be advanced if some family characteristics were weeded out of the ol' gene patch. Others are not as offensive, and some could be called downright pleasing.

Hayden Sharp

Hayden is one grandchild in whom I see similarities to myself, and that's not necessarily good for either of us. Much of the time Hayden is somewhat unkempt. One would think that his role model is Pigpen of Peanuts fame. His pants are torn, dirt stains abound, shoes untied, and, if wearing socks, they are not mates. Which shoe goes on which foot was never a problem for him in the past–he didn't care. But I noticed a breakthrough on a recent visit: the shoes, although still untied, had found their rightful feet.

Hayden, like many children, had a favorite "blankee" that eventually was reduced to a rag. He retained this treasure much too long. It was last seen (by the family) when he forgot and left it in the bed covers at a hotel while on vacation. Apparently, it was gathered up by the maid with all the sheets and taken to the laundry. There was a search but it was never found. Can't you imagine the conversation between the housekeepers at break time?

"How was your morning?"

"Not bad, in fact, good, I found thirty-seven cents!"

"And your morning?"

"Great, I found what appears to be a fragment of the Shroud of Turin. It's being carbon dated as we speak."

46

Hayden is a loving and a lovable boy. His facial expressions and eyes can cause an urge in one that can only be satisfied with a hug. I doubt he gets the same satisfaction as I do from those embraces. I know they will be fewer, possibly none, as he approaches the teens. He has adopted Marynelle, greets her when she enters his home, and takes her around showing the latest changes to his house, his room or whatever. He shows great affection toward her. I like seeing them together. Hayden cares deeply for his older brother Trevor although many of their interests differ. None-the-less, it is not unusual to hear him ask, "Where's Trevor?" after which he goes off looking.

Hayden showed an early interest in sports and it has not lessened. This is where I see myself in him. My interest was self-generated for there was no one pushing me, and Hayden's parents are not pushing him. He pushes them. When I visit, only a few minutes will go by before he says, "Do you want to play pass?" which in my youth was, "Do you want to play catch?" At eight years old baseball is his favorite sport and he has an arm I envy. I'm amazed at his awareness of where to play, his covering of bases, his ability to hit. He also plays tennis and basketball, but baseball is his real love. That is evidenced by the condition of the backyard which his father had so carefully brought to a beautiful green a few years ago. Now, only a few tufts of grass remain, and they will go the way of the others if the boys persist on playing ball during the winter.

One of my favorite stories about Hayden was when he accompanied his mother each day to pick up Trevor at school. When they arrived, the fourth grade boys would be playing football. Hayden was four and I don't know if he struck up an acquaintance with the boys (the most believable version) or they saw him peering through the fence and invited him to play. Throughout that year Hayden played football with the fourth graders while awaiting his brother's dismissal from school. That relationship with the older boys continues today as he sits on their bench during baseball season; that is, when he isn't playing in his league.

When Hayden enters school each day he speaks to each of his classmates by name. He has been known to require a response if none is forthcoming. He is so gregarious that one teacher thought he would be a politician. He'll get my vote, but only if his shoes are on the right feet.

April 2004

YELLOWSTONE ON THE CHEAP

It was in the spring of 1991 when Joe and Nancy Vanderglas asked me to go with them for a quick trip to the Tetons and Yellowstone. I had just lost my wife, Pat, so I suspected they wanted to shake me out of my doldrums. I questioned why they wanted to spoil a vacation by having an extra man along, but they insisted. I'm glad they did.

The trip was short, but one that whetted my desire to spend more time in the park: to see it in greater detail, to get off the road and into the back country, to hike, to slow down, to have a real park experience. The first opportunity to return to the park was in 1994. My working career had come to an end. I had worked myself out of a job at LOGTEC; no longer was I needed. At age sixty-one it was time to play.

In Yellowstone with Joe and Nancy, I noticed the number of older people working in the stores—men and women who were on AARP's mailing list and some that had a Medicare card in their wallets. I asked one about employment and he promptly handed me an application. I took it home and set it aside for the day I might use it. I was unwilling to spend a couple of months in the park using my dollars. The best alternative was to apply for a job with Hamilton Stores and hope there was enough time off to explore the park.

In the spring of 1994 I pulled out the Hamilton Store's application, filled it out, and mailed it. I could have worked all summer and up until October. However, I was concerned about such a long time, possibly in a job that soured the whole park experience. Five months was too long. With that in mind, I told Hamilton that I could be there August 1 and work until the store closed for the season. I knew that many employees would be college students and returning to school in August and September. This proved to be accurate. Hamilton Stores told me to report August 10 for the remainder of the season. Even if the job proved terrible, I could handle two months.

I was assigned to the Canyon Store, which as the name indicates, was near the Yellowstone River Canyon and the waterfalls. The store had a short-order grill, sections for jewelry, souvenirs, clothing, sports, and groceries. All were small, tailored to the tourist/camper/outdoors person. I was placed in the grocery: stocking shelves, unloading trucks, waiting on customers, and occasionally, manning the cash register/ checkout. At the latter task I proved less than capable. The equipment was of the pre-scanner era which required keying in the individual items. I had to look at the keys, had trouble finding price tags, trouble reading them when found, and invariably the register tape would clog or be used up when I was there. A veteran would have to step in and correct the problem. A veteran may be someone who had been hired a week before you. There were two bosses, both retired Navy men, large, in good shape, and careful never to ask me to place fifty pound cartons over my head on the third shelf in the storage room. I appreciated that very much.

The store was open from 7:00 a.m. to 9:00 p.m. There were two crews; each worked in 3 1/2 hour shifts with a 3 1/2 hour break during the day. This allowed time to hike, go to the falls, fish, sight-see, or whatever. I'm confident the company had looked at the ages of some and knew siestas would be required to keep us alert, thus the 3 1/2 hour shifts.

The store's business was feast or famine. Until Labor Day it was very busy. After the holiday the crowds lessened considerably. The greatest number of customers occurred when bus tours would stop. Popular souvenirs were small figurines of bears, moose, elk and bison mounted on cedar bases. These little jewels were popular with seniors and particularly Asians arriving on the tours. Something for the coffee table at home, I suppose. Our ice cream counter was near the front of the store where the attendant could see the parking lot. When a bus pulled up, he would yell, "Cedar alert, cedar alert," for all to hear. All sections in the store would prepare for the onslaught. I didn't know what Ramen noodles were until I worked in the grocery. We couldn't keep the noodles on the shelf when the West Coast tours stopped by. The hot water supply in the rest rooms was exhausted while the bus idled, awaiting its passengers.

I found the meals provided by Hamilton quite adequate. Possibly it was because I had tired of my attempts at cooking while at home. Many complained about the food, but they had been there since the store opened in May and had tired of the repetitiveness of the menu. Also, many were "meat and potatoes" people for whom casseroles fell short. A big event was for a party of people to drive 50 miles outside the park to a café to eat steak. I did it a couple of times, but felt the beef had come straight off the range without benefit of a feed lot. It was the idea of getting away for awhile that was so appealing.

We stayed in a barracks-like place–married couples at one end, single men and women on separate floors. I had to share my room with a college student for a few nights. He moved out, I'm sure because of the generational gap between us, and for which I was relieved. My room was so dusty that I'm sure some of it dated to when Teddy Roosevelt visited. I spent little time there, mostly just to sleep. Down the hall was a bathroom shared by all the single men.

I broke a rule by hiking by myself much of the time. It was recommended that you hike with at least one other person for safety reasons. Grizzlies were a concern. To counter this threat, pepper spray and a tingling bell were standard items on every hike. Bears are the most dangerous when startled; therefore, a bell pinned on one's pack was a necessity. Supposedly, hearing the bell was enough for the bear to depart the area. It must have worked because I never encountered one. And I never spotted a bell in a bears' scat either. The only bears seen during my two months in the park were a mother and two cubs, too far off to be a danger.

My first hike was to a remote lake to do some exploring. It was in an area where the woods were quite thick, too dense to see through. I was ducking branches, struggling through undergrowth making a lot of racket. I stopped to listen. I was not alone. There was something nearby also making a lot of noise as it plodded through the woods. I froze and peered as hard as I could in the direction of the footfalls. Suddenly a cow moose and her calf appeared a few feet away. I eased my way out of there making certain not to get between the two.

On one hike into the backcountry, I met a couple who stopped me and said there was a mule up ahead on the trail. What would a mule be doing in the park? Had it escaped from a trailer? I thought of burros and the possibility it was a descendant of an old miner's pack animal, but the park had not been mined. As I hiked along, mulling over the mule's presence, I came upon a yearling moose. It was about the size of a mule, and without antlers it somewhat resembled one. Mystery solved.

A retired professor ran the sports section of the store. Ben was an expert on fly fishing and was sought by many an angler who visited the park. I watched him fish one day in a stream in the Lamar Valley. Convinced I could master this art, I had him set me up with some gear. I caught a few trout at different times, but no records. On one of the last days in September, Joe from Florida and I set out along the Yellowstone River. It was a day when winter was in the air; an occasional snow-flake made an appearance. Joe was a serious fisherman at home, but fly fishing was not something he did along the Atlantic. We fished for four hours and struck out—zilch. The next day a man came into the store, headed for the sports section and told Ben he had a great day yesterday along the Yellowstone. He had caught several large trout. Ben asked, "Where?" The man named the stretch of river on which Joe and I had fished.

Today, the fly rod gathers dust.

Away from the crowds, and on a mountain or along a stream, Yellowstone was a spiritual experience. It had a calming effect—an effect that would cause a reflective mood. A favorite retreat was by the rapids on the Yellowstone River. It was tree-lined, cool in the heat of the day, and the rapids served as a stage for the Harlequins, ducks that would quickly fly upstream to the top of the rapids, land on the water, and go under. They would not reappear until the river had carried them to the bottom of the rapids—a trip of 70 yards. I never learned if they were feeding while on their underwater journey or just having fun. Either way, the Harlequins were always good for a show.

Before I left, to return to Ohio, the elk went into their rutting season. Several "families" congregated in an area nearby. It was quite interesting to see the courtship that took place and how the bulls controlled their harems. A cow would wander off but not for long. The bull would make his bugling sound, go after her, round her up, and herd her back to his courting area. The edge of the clearing in the woods was lined with wildlife photographers. The elk should have sold tickets.

Several times I drove out of the park to see other places of interest: Cody, Red Lodge, the Beartooth Mountains, and Virginia City were visited. One of the most interesting was the area where the earthquake occurred in 1959. To stand on ground high above the Madison River, a river dammed up by the quake, was eerie knowing that buried one hundred feet below, were bodies never recovered. Twenty-four people, most of whom were campers, perished that night.

The Park embraced September. Nights turned crisp, mornings dawned frosty, aspens became golden, thin sheets of ice formed along streams' edges. I helped close the store for the season.

Yellowstone may have been done "on the cheap," but I left "wealthy," at peace, content, rejuvenated.

December 2004

LINE CALLS

I play tennis. Mind you, it's not the kind of tennis you see when Wimbledon or the U.S. Open appears on the tube. It's a significantly diluted version of the pro game. I play the kind of tennis that can lull a person to sleep. I call it "old man's" tennis, no relevance to my age, though I qualify, but rather to my style of play. It is a style played since I started the game in my twenties.

I'm a retriever. I don't hit with a lot of pace, don't hit winning shots, but try to keep the ball in play, awaiting an error by my opponent. The only thing I have in common with the big boys is that we both play on courts with like dimensions. Playing the "old man's" style is okay when you are younger, have a cardiovascular system of a horse and legs that are alive. Today, I have none of these attributes, so winning comes less often. To win today I must carefully select my opponents, choosing only those with arthritic backs who have both knees wrapped. If my opponent brings along an oxygen tank, that's a plus.

But, this is not about my game or lack thereof; this is about an interesting aspect of tennis, specifically, "line calls." At the level of tennis we play there are no officials. The players are responsible for making the calls when a ball is out. How players handle this responsibility is what makes tennis a study in human frailties. In singles, just two people are saddled with this responsibility. The frailties increase exponentially when playing doubles.

Competition does funny things to some people and tennis can be a stage for observing those funny things. For some, competition brings out traits buried deep inside. Traits that haven't surfaced since man first decided to stand upright. I find it fascinating to observe a particular man, otherwise mild-mannered, whose public aura would have you believe he served as Mother Teresa's guru, but on the court his temperament becomes a hybrid of John McEnroe's and Ilie Nastase's. He questions every line call, has the court etiquette of a love-crazed gorilla, and refuses to buy beer afterwards. Not my favorite fellow.

Without officials, a good practice to follow (rarely used by those with whom I play), is to assume all shots are good unless you *SEE THEM OUT.* If it is not *SEEN OUT,* it is *IN.* This followed faithfully means there are no, "I didn't see it" or "I'm not sure whether it was good or not" calls. In both the latter situations the shots are *GOOD!*

Nothing is more discouraging than to play a long 10-minute rally of pitty-pat returns at which point you gather enough strength to hit a winning shot, a shot that is clearly *IN.* However, your opponent takes that moment of euphoria away by saying, "I'm not sure if it was in or not. Let's play it over." He, of course, is not interested in following the *SEE IT OUT* principle. I, being totally exhausted, am unable to respond, since I am off court, behind a tree, giving up last night's enchiladas.

Possibly some examples will help in understanding the "line call" phenomena. A common one is for you opponent, Laser Eye Leonard, to hit a ball to your end of the court and question your "out" call. He does this despite being eighty feet away from the line on which you are standing. Your "out" call is being questioned by a man who last saw the big "E" on the eye chart 15 years ago. There are a variety of ways the call may be questioned by Laser Eye.

> 1-He denigrates your eyesight. Your verbal rejoinder, accompanied by an appropriate gesture, will dictate the tenor of the match from that point on–that is, if the match goes on.

> 2-Laser Eye stands and stares at the spot where the ball landed, sending the message, "You gotta be kiddin'." You may react in a number of ways, but probably the most effective is to ignore the stare and get ready for the next point. If you want to be really devious, add a small smile to your face, the kind of smile that says, "I know something you don't." This tactic has been known to cause some players to seek therapy.

> 3-Or he may ask, "How far was it out?"–thereby sending the message, "You gotta be kiddin'." At this point you

might hold up your thumb and forefinger indicating how far the ball was out by the distance between the two digits. This is a risky response which leaves the door open for the kind of dialogue found unacceptable in diplomatic channels. An effective way of stopping further questioning is to announce the distance the ball was out in fractions of inches; e.g., "It was out 1 and 15/16 inches" or "2 and 7/8 inches." A response of this preciseness can cause some opponents to lose their concentration, possibly distract them to the point of losing the match.

Then there is the player that views his racket as a howitzer. Ol'Artillery Arthur uses his warm-up as if to sight in his weapon. He slams the ball as hard as he can, than asks you how far out was the ball. He isn't questioning whether it was out or not: rather he is using you as his forward observer. In his mind you are providing him coordinates that will enable him to shell the enemy. All this occurs during warm-ups in which you do not get a chance to warm-up. Your time is spent dodging his salvos. This player tends to calm down somewhat during actual play. However, he can easily morph into the McEnroe/Nastase hybrid if his howitzer misfires and you call the shot out.

Occasionally a ball is hit down the line on your side of the net. The ball is out but you, standing at a right angle to where it landed, are not in a good position to make the call. You believe the ball is out but following the rule–you must *SEE IT OUT,* do not make the call. Your opponent, looking down the line, is in the best position to see where the ball landed on you side. Several possibilities can occur:

1-Your opponent, being a good sport, not a win-at-all-cost type, calls the ball out giving you the point.

2-Your opponent, being a win-at-all-cost type, turns his back and goes into position for the next point. You may ask him if the shot was in hoping for a pang of conscience to strike. It is important how you frame the question. It is harder for him to say, "It was not in," than to nod yes to your question, "Was it out?"

3-A really hard-nosed opponent will say, "You call your side, I'll call mine." These types are few and far between, but when they come around they rank right up there with the player that refuses to buy the beer.

Those are a few of the line-call situations I have experienced. I have not even touched on the kind of calls that can arise on serves. Pros can hit first serves in the 130 mile per hour range. They have far less controversy on whether a ball was in or out than my friends and I do on our 30 mile per hour serves. Why is that? That's a topic for another time. I must go now or I'll be late for my match with Laser Eye!

January 2005

ELLE

I see humor in little kids. Of course, it is important that they don't see you see humor in them. The belly laugh has to be stifled until you leave the room. Only then, out of the little dears' presence, can you guffaw. You don't want to create a little monster.

My granddaughter Elle is not a monster. In fact her Granddad has a "crush" on her. She's a little "knockout." When Elle is old enough to read this, her mother will have to assure her that those are two terms old people used back in the mid 20th century. Let's hope her mother gives it a positive spin for "crush" and "knockout" were not around in Jill's era either.

Elle is six, in the first grade, loves it and is irritated when Saturday arrives. How long will that attitude last?

Elle is my youngest grandchild. Because of the distance between us we have spent less time together than a granddad prefers. So, much of what will be in here was provided by her mother. That's okay because Jill and I tend to have the same sense of humor. I'll trust her mother's selection of Elle's view of the world about her.

These occurred from the age of three to five and a half.

One day Jill checked the cleanliness of Elle's bathroom. Among other things there was toothpaste smeared on the counter and the cap was off the tube. Jill told Elle how important it was to keep the bathroom clean and she could start by cleaning up the mess on the counter. Elle retorted with, "Who do you think I am, Cinderella?" Obviously she had watched that movie one too many times.

Elle stuck out her tongue when teased by her brother. She was caught in the act by her mother. When being reprimanded, Elle replied, "I was just giving it some air."

"Mom, you're getting on my nurse (nerves)."

Jill was a nurse and worked for Dr. Singh, a Sikh with the typical beard and turban. Elle asked Dr. Singh, "How can you eat with that beard on?"

When seeing her mother in some stage of being less than fully dressed, Elle observed, "Mom, you've got a 'jiggery' bottom."

One time fearing a spanking she pleaded, "Don't spank my bottom."

Jill: "Why"

Elle: "Because it's a good bottom."

Jill: "Why."

Elle: "Because it always has a smile on it."

There was no spanking!

Elle Buffenbarger

Elle from a very young age has been into waitressing. She would go around the room with a piece of paper, an imaginary pencil taking each person's order. Shortly, she would return with the orders "filled."

She was at my 70th birthday party, really in her element, for there were thirty people there for her to wait on and she did a great job at four years of age. One man's coffee was not forthcoming from the kitchen and he kiddingly asked her when it was going to be served. She went into the kitchen and in an authoritative voice said, "That man out there wants his coffee NOW."

Her mother visited her for lunch at school one day. The lunchroom was filled with noisy first graders, too noisy for the lunchroom monitors. When one monitor began asking for quiet over the din, Elle commented to those around her, "Duh, we are children you know."

When she announced to her grandmother that she had three boyfriends, her grandmother asked if she could have just one of them. Elle quashed that with, "Duh, they ARE preschoolers." There's that "duh" again, an expression disliked by many adults (mostly seniors).

Elle went with her father, mother, and brother to a restaurant. The waitress, a candidate for the "Let's Reduce Obesity in America" program, arrived at the table to take orders. Elle, knowing that babies resided in mommy's "stomach," asked the young woman if she were going to have a baby. The question was ignored while Elle's family squirmed. Elle was persistent until a "NO" reply was forthcoming. Her family, having been unsuccessful in diverting the topic elsewhere, had to be dug out from under the table.

Elle and her family attend a church where immersion is part of the baptismal ceremony. Elle had witnessed this on several occasions including her brother's baptism. We are uncertain if that triggered her desire to be baptized or if it was in some of the Sunday School lessons, but she put pressure on the minister to be baptized. He felt she was too young to understand its meaning and shared that with her parents. Elle was undeterred. She continued to frequently broach the topic to the minister. He gave in and had a baptismal ceremony with the family present.

This child is fun!! I want to be around in fifteen years to see if the dogged pursuit and confidence she exhibits today is present then. If it remains, there will be no denying her. Maybe she will be doing the baptisms!

March 2005

"54,896"

Every municipality in Belgium appears to have a memorial to soldiers who died in World War I. The memorials, standing silent, by their presence alone, speak to the carnage of that war. It was a war that lasted four long years until the armistice in 1918.

Through the history of Europe and its wars, Belgium seems to be the land opposing forces selected for their conflicts. Its location and terrain lends itself to being a suitable arena for war-making. Possibly if the Belgians could borrow a few Alps from the Swiss, Belgium, too, might become difficult to penetrate. Future combatants would be forced to go elsewhere or maybe do something novel–not go to war.

Ieper is ten miles from France and thirty miles from the North Sea in the Flanders region. Populated with nearly thirty thousand people, it is like most towns and villages in Western Europe featuring a market center or town square around which business, government, pleasure, and church all reside.

Battles were fought in and around Ieper between 1914 and 1918. A strategic location, it became a primary target for bombardments. The town's structures could not withstand the cannons' pounding. The church on the town plaza was destroyed and the Cloth Hall had but a piece of a wall standing when hostilities ended. The hall derived its name from its role in the Middle Ages as a leading manufacturing and weaving center for cloth. The building is very large, nearly one hundred thirty yards along the sides, and with its tower nearly eight stories high. It is quite substantial, typical of construction used in the past in Europe: masonry, stone and brick.

After the war, the hall and all of the town's structures were rebuilt. Today, the Cloth Hall houses a museum to the war years and a visitors'center.

The British suffered greatly at Ieper. They lost three hundred twenty-five thousand soldiers in the Flanders fields in and around the town. Today, there are one hundred thirty-four cemeteries in the area which are the final resting place for soldiers from the British Empire–some with few graves and some with thousands.

Mennin Gate

Meninstraat is one of the major streets providing entry to the town. Before it reaches the town center, it passes through the Mennin Gate, a structure thirty-six yards long and twenty yards wide. This large marble arch is a memorial to the British soldiers that fought at Ieper but were never identified for burial in a marked grave. On the walls of the memorial and the ceiling arching overhead were engraved 54,896 names. That bears repeating: 54,896 killed whose remains were never identified. How, after such a loss, could Europe let itself be drawn into an even larger war twenty years later?

Every evening at 8:00 p.m., the Ieper Volunteer Fire Brigade's band recognizes the British contribution with a brief ceremony at the Mennin Gate. After the ceremony they turn and march to the town square playing music followed by a small contingent of uniformed veterans, visitors, and townspeople. Ben, Marion, Marynelle, and I followed as well.

The memorial gate, those etched names that went on and on, the committed little band, the veterans, and the approximately five hundred visitors evoked a contemplative reverence.

A poem, recited by many of us as school children, calls for repeating here. It was written in 1915 by John McCrae, a Canadian soldier who fought in Flanders.

In Flanders Fields
In Flanders fields the poppies blow
Between the crosses, row on row
That mark our place; and in the sky
The larks, still bravely singing, fly
Scarce heard amid the guns below.
We are the Dead. Short days ago
We lived, felt dawn, saw sunset glow,
Loved and were loved, and now we lie
In Flanders fields.

Take up our quarrel with the foe
To you from failing hands we throw
The torch; be yours to hold it high.
If ye break faith with us who die
We shall not sleep, though poppies grow
In Flanders fields.

May 2005

THE NUDGE

Beneath the cover of darkness,
Under a layer of quilt,
It arrived, minus sound,
The Nudge in the night.

Could it be love's touch,
With suggestion to follow?
Nudge meant no such,
But, turn, Dear—snore not!

September 2005

Trevor Petersen and Grandmother Bucky

Sharp and Greene Children - David, Todd, Ben, Kelli, Jill

Wedding Day – January 2001

Trevor and Hayden Sharp with Granddad

Seth and Elle Buffenbarger

THE MARRYIN' SQUIRE

When you delve into genealogy be ready for an occasional surprise. There could be a derelict uncle which your mother passed over when sharing family stories. Or your father failed to mention a great grandfather that managed two households when your family only knew of one–yours. Then there are the renegades, the ones that may have operated on the wrong side of the law. Many of us rather like the law-breaker as long as he/she is several generations back, out of reach of people's memories. It can't be someone near to you on the tree like a grandfather or aunt. That's much too close. For some, finding a Billy the Kid or a Jesse James in the ancestral tree is like discovering a genealogy golden nugget.

My mother was a Shelton. There was a Shelton Gang in downstate Illinois that thrived during the 1920s and 30s. They began operating when prohibition became law and expanded into gambling and prostitution. No one was ever able to make a familial connection between Mom's clan and the gang in Illinois. But if you lived in Illinois and had the name Shelton it was a given that you were in cahoots with them.

Uncle Dode Shelton lived near Farmington, Illinois. He worked in the strip mines nearby. There were people suspicious of him. They weren't listening when he would say, "No, I moved here from Ohio. I've never lived in southern Illinois." It didn't help Dode's cause when one of the gang, Bernie Shelton, was gunned down entering a nearby Farmington tavern.

Uncle Claude Shelton told the story of when he accompanied his brother Dwight on a trip to the Farmington mines in the 1930s. Dwight was an executive with the Marion Steam Shovel and was responsible for sales of the large excavators. The brothers drove out from Ohio and registered in a Peoria hotel using aliases. They knew better than to write "Shelton" on the pad.

No evidence tying the Illinois gang to my "gang" of Sheltons has been found. However, my Sheltons do have a character way back in early Ohio. Thomas Shelton didn't serve any jail time but there were

69

Squire Thomas Shelton

many who thought it was a good idea. He had quite a reputation along the Ohio River for some forty-five years. He was widely known in southern Ohio and northern Kentucky. Certainly, there were many that he made happy for he married thousands during his long tenure as a Justice of Peace. And it is just as certain there had to be hundreds, maybe thousands, who were very unhappy with him.

Thomas Shelton is my great-great-great-grandfather. He lived in Aberdeen, Ohio, across the Ohio River from the pretty town of Maysville, Kentucky. Aberdeen resided in Huntington Township and in 1822 Thomas Shelton began his forty-eight year career as a Justice of Peace. The term "squire" was generally applied to the justice of peace position, a term brought to the colonies in the 1600s by the Scottish and English settlers. "Squire" continued in use into the 1800's. In Ohio, the position was involved with taxing, building roads, schools, court matters, maintaining the peace.

Squire Shelton must have been somewhat bored as the Justice of Peace for he went into the marrying industry in a big way. The Squire's entrepreneurial instincts kicked in soon after being elected to the office. Aberdeen became the destination for marriages, both hurried ones and ones that did not require a shotgun. Aberdeen's reputation grew until it began to be called the "Gretna Green of America." Gretna Green was a Scottish village on the English border that became a haven in the 1700s for English couples wanting to marry. They were escaping the more restrictive marriage laws of England by going into Scotland.

Aberdeen, Ohio was in an ideal location for travelers in the 1800s. The Ohio River was a major artery for the movement of goods and people. It was a stop on the Cincinnati to Pittsburgh steamboat run, a terminus for the Zane Trace, an early road in the Ohio country and it was across the river from a major Kentucky port of commerce, Maysville. It was not long before the railroads added to the town's accessibility.

People from all walks of life came to Aberdeen to be married by Squire Shelton. Some might arrive in fine dress with a handsome team pulling a fancy carriage. Others might arrive on foot and stand in front of the Squire with those feet bared. Couples came from all over the South, from Pennsylvania, New York, Indiana, Illinois and Missouri. Probably the state most heavily represented was Kentucky, for that state required a marriage bond before the nuptials. Shelton even conducted marriages for a few runaway slaves; slaves using the underground railroad through Ohio into Canada. There was pounding on Shelton's door one night. He arose from bed to check on the ruckus. An excited young man demanded to be married right then, for the irate father and brothers of the bride were in hot pursuit on horseback. The Squire, in his nightshirt, married them on the street outside his house and went back to bed. It seems he required nothing more than two warm bodies and some sort of payment. Few questions were asked of the couples.

Shelton would walk to the wharf anytime the paddle wheeler's whistle announced its arrival. If a couple got off to be married he would conduct the ceremony on the dock. He would intone, "Marriage is an ordinance, instituted by an all-wise Jehovah. Jine yer right hands. Do you take this woman to nourish and cherish, to keep her in sickness and health? I hope you live long and do well together. Take your seats."

The Squire was paid in whatever the couple could afford. His pockets bulged and if payment was pork, garden produce, or a watch they would be placed in his "store" for his use, for sale, or bartering. One couple, unable to pay, told Shelton that they had a good crop of potatoes in the ground and when ready to dig up they would bring them to him in payment. The Squire agreed. The couple carried the potatoes to Aberdeen on foot in baskets for their lone horse had died shortly after the wedding. They made several trips to complete the agreement. Apparently, the man did not rue the agreement for ten years later he called upon Shelton for his services again. His first wife had died. No potato payment this time. He paid for the second wedding with a $20 gold piece.

There is no clear picture of how many weddings Thomas Shelton conducted. He didn't know and his record keeping was sporadic at best. The *Adams and Brown Counties History of 1880* states that he officiated at over 4000 marriages. "Hundreds of young people whose parents were unfavorable to their plans, flew to the old "Squire" and found his services an efficient remedy for their misfortunes. He always claimed that the majority of his marriages were happily made, and if they turned out to the contrary, he consoled himself with the reflection that his own part was well done, and he was not to blame."

Aberdeen loved their Squire. The December 16, 1857 *Maysville Eagle* reported: "Squire Shelton Reelected. For the encouragement and comfort of runaway couples, and of love-sick young folks who want to make runaway couples, we take pleasure in chronicling the important fact that their old favorite Thomas Shelton, was, on yesterday, reelected to the post of Esquire or Justice of the Peace for Huntington Township, Ohio , opposite this city. His plurality was forty-one over two opponents, Massie Beasley and Zenos Cooper Jr." Thomas Shelton continued to be re-elected until his death in 1870.

Aberdeen was twenty miles from the county seat of Georgetown where the marriages were to be registered. Some were and some were not. Maybe the Squire was too busy officiating to take the time to go to the courthouse. After all, he could conduct several marriages in the time it took to make a forty mile round trip to the county seat. So, the legality of many marriages would come into question. Some families had several generations married by the Squire raising the possibility that entire families could be cohabitating illegally.

The lid blew off after the Civil War when children and widows of the soldiers were applying for pensions. Evidence of marriage to the veteran was required. One can imagine the flood of mail coming into Aberdeen and the little courthouse in Georgetown. Kentucky was hit the hardest with the veteran's issue. So universal were the numbers in Kentucky that the legislature passed a law legitimizing all marriages of their citizens that had been conducted by Squire Thomas Shelton of Aberdeen. Probably the biggest furor over the veterans' pensions was sometime after Shelton's death. There were many laws passed on behalf of the veterans and their families after 1870.

The Squire was nearly 100 when he died. He had been widowed fifteen years. He had fathered eleven children. Jeremiah, his eighth child, was born May 17, 1813. Jeremiah, my great-great-grandfather, married Elizabeth Prather July 15, 1834. Jeremiah and Elizabeth were unlike the couples who came from hundreds of miles around to be married by the Squire. They were married in Pike County, Ohio.

For whatever reason, Jeremiah and Elizabeth didn't travel the fifty miles down to Aberdeen to be married by his father. Possibly Jeremiah was aware of the Ol' Squire's laxity in record keeping. Elizabeth and Jeremiah wanted to assure a record existed of their union. They wanted to be legit.

October 2005

Resources:

Henry Howe, "Adams and Brown Counties History of 1880" Ohio
"Southern Ohio Gretna Green," *Louisville Courier Journal*, 4 August, 1897

Randy McNutt, "Marrying Kind," *Ohio Magazine* (April, 1994)

NATE'S LITTLE BLACK BOOKS

I struck gold last week. Cousin Ann, knowing of my interest in family lore, sent me a packet containing some of her father's little black books. They were not black books with the phone numbers of Uncle Nate's love interests. They contained cryptic notes of money spent, for what and how much. The writing was tiny but legible. It had to be tiny–the books were shirt-pocket size–2 ¾ by 4 ¼ inches.

Looking at these books, I'm amazed how a ledger entry with its related cost can cause memories to bubble to the top. Not only do you reflect on an uncle's life, but on your own as well.

Rarely did a day go by without some entry in the books. And Nate had a coding system which permitted a stratification of expenses. Every entry had a number code and the two remained consistent throughout. Some numbers like two (2) and three (3) never appear. They probably were used initially but over time those entries became extraneous. The forty-eight entries in October, 1929 included:

DATE	ENTRY	CODE	COST
Oct 1	board, room, and washing	1	$46.00
Oct 1	paper and magazine	9	.29
Oct 11	barber	4	.50
Oct 11	baseball pool	20	.50
Oct 20	theater	12	1.00
Oct 25	gas 7 gal	6	1.54
Oct 26	Esther	20	1.00

Each month started off with the **board, room and washing** entry. Nate was a twenty-nine-year-old bachelor in 1929 living in Marion, Ohio. He was employed at the Marion Steam Shovel Company.

The **paper and magazine** purchase is a fond memory. There were always interesting publications to read when visiting this favorite relative. *Life Magazine* with its World War II scenes and *National Geographic* were must reads for me. And sometimes the Sunday *Columbus Dispatch* was lying in the sunroom.

The little black books tell us that Nate visited the barber each week, something I find difficult to believe. I try to make it once a month to the barber. He was always well-groomed and now I know why.

Nate Shelton

It was obviously World Series time, and Nate was in an office pool. He was an ardent Yankee fan. Nate would tease me about how his Yankees were superior to my Indians. He may have made me a Yankee-hater. I don't follow the game as closely today but my dislike for the Yankees remains.

The theater entry would usually appear twice a month. Occasionally, "wrestling" would replace the second show. Both found a home under code 20. Wow, gas for 22 cents a gallon! I'm confident none of it came from the Mideast in 1929. Nate consistently gave my Aunt Esther (his sister) one dollar a week. Why, I'm not sure. I do know the brothers and sisters looked out for each other—Aunt Esther raised her sisters (Ferne, my mother, and Edith) from the ages of twelve and nine, respectively. Possibly, it was a small contribution which was combined with monies provided by other siblings. Looking back, I never appreciated how the brothers and sisters, eleven in all, cared and supported each other. It is a story waiting to be told.

Gigantic Bank Pool Pledged to Avert Disaster as Second Big Crash Stuns Wall Street

The New York World's headline,
October 29, 1929.

Stock Market Will Close for Two Days

The Marion Star headline Nate would
have seen, October 30, 1929.

Black Tuesday had hit. The stock market crashed never to return to its October, 1929 levels until 1954. Nate's recording of his expenses stopped on October 27 and he did not list his expenses again until November 1. It was unusual for him to stop recording his costs for such a long period. Could it have been the shock of the market news?

DATE	ENTRY	CODE	COST
Nov 1	Board, room and washing	1	$46.00
Nov 4	paper and magazine	9	.45
Nov 8	barber	4	.50
Nov 16	theater	12	1.00
Nov 21	gas 10 gal	6	2.10

We have all seen those movie depictions of people doing desperate things after the October 1929 crash, the most desperate being jumping off tall buildings. You see no such desperation in Nate's ledgers. The entries, their codes and the costs remained consistently the same in November and on into 1930. He was still going to the barber once a week, seeing movies, and driving his car. His landlady apparently wasn't worried about losing a customer. She charged the same $46.00. I learned later that his "landlady" was actually his sister, my Aunt Ethel Welch. Despite the terrible economic news, Nate's expenditures, and presumably his income, remained the same in 1930.

Leafing through 1930 I saw three entries that caught my eye:

DATE	ENTRY	CODE	COST
Nov 21	marriage license	20	$2.50
Nov 21	minister	20	5.00
Nov 21	ring	14	15.00

Uncle Nate and Aunt Helen were married right after the Ohio State-Michigan football game November 22. They had their priorities, football first, marriage second. Two days later there was an expenditure of $3.90 for cigars. The office would have been blue with smoke as the men celebrated with the new groom. Earlier in November, Nate had bought a chance on a turkey and stamped the code **20** on this little adventure in gambling. I smile to think a chance on a turkey fits in the same category as paying a minister to conduct marriage nuptials. And the marriage license was thrown in code **20** for good measure.

One thing for sure—the marriage was no turkey. It was a definite winner. Aunt Helen and I were always close.

By 1944 Nate's recordings were of events. Cost data no longer were being entered into the little books. Had they found residency elsewhere or was such precise cost collection no longer a need? Or maybe they moved to a book that Aunt Helen kept. Some entries in 1944:

January 30, 1944, Went to Chick's, Doc's grave

January 30, 1944 was a Sunday. Sunday was the day to visit others or have visitors. Some visits were expected but most were "spur of the moment" drop-ins. Visits were a welcome distraction for those living in the semi-isolation of rural Ohio during World War II.

Chick was Uncle Claude, Nate's brother, who lived on a farm near Iberia, Ohio. The only people I ever heard call him Chick were his older brothers and sisters. It must have been a boyhood nickname, reserved for use by those closest to him. In our house he was always Claude.

Uncle Claude's farm was very close to town. The town cemetery was in a pretty setting on a hill overlooking his farm. Dwight (Doc) was the oldest of the brothers and sisters. He had died suddenly the previous March at fifty-six years. He was president of the Marion Steam Shovel Company, a company experiencing labor problems while trying to maintain wartime production. The family believed it was a stress-induced heart attack.

February 4, 1944, Claridon 34, Prospect 17

Nate and Helen's daughter Ann went to the Claridon High School which was always at or near the top among our county schools in basketball. For many years my school, New Bloomington, took it on the chin from Claridon and I would hear about it. Later, when I played, I always felt Nate was quietly wanting my school to win–maybe I'm wrong, but I'd like to believe that. We managed to beat Claridon my junior and senior years but Ann was already in college. She was elsewhere, her interests were elsewhere, and nowhere near for me to indulge in some revengeful teasing.

February 20, 1944, Went Over to Ferne's

Ferne's meant a Sunday visit to our house. It would have been in the afternoon. In 1944, during the war, gas rationing limited drives for pleasure. But the fuel required to make the seventeen-mile jaunt to our house was not a lot. When a vehicle came down the road from the east, it could be heard as it approached the small grade a third of a mile away. The grade was too small to qualify as a hill, but it did provide an added boost to an old car's speed and announced its arrival. Each vehicle had its own signature provided by the noise it made. It could be a noise an old muffler no longer muffled, a clattering engine, valves tapping or all three. A car going west each day after work in a Marion factory could be identified by sound alone. You might not know the driver, but you recognized the car, its make and year. Everyone waved whether you knew them or not.

When Uncle Nate, Aunt Helen and Ann would come on a Sunday, the well-tuned Chrysler would not give away their arrival until it had nearly reached our driveway. It was a "see-before-hear vehicle," unlike those passing the house during the week.

I looked forward to those visits. Sometimes some old magazines would come with them. There would probably be some teasing about my school's poor basketball team or about girls which would at eleven years of age make me squirm, try to change the subject, or look for an escape route.

June 6, 1944, Allies invaded Europe between LeHavre and Cherbourg inFrance

Nate was a reader who kept up with current affairs. The news of the Normandy landing could have been gleaned from The Marion Star or possibly from an Edward R. Murrow radio broadcast. Regardless, it was apparent the Allies had a foothold that would provide the impetus for a push into Germany. Certainly it justified recording in the 1944 little black book.

July 2, 1944, Ned came for a week

Visiting relatives for a week in the summer was always a welcome break. Kids don't seem to do this today as my generation once did. Maybe adult-organized activities capture too many of those valuable summer days leaving little time for the Uncle Nates and Aunt Helens of today. They lived in the country as we did, but their place provided a different variety of activities than my home. It relieved the boredom of summer and provided an escape from mowing yards. It was always a fun week although I missed playing baseball and basketball. Cousin Ann had no interest in trying to hit my fast ball.

So many thoughts emerge when reading the entries in Nate's books. Slipping back into the past when reading them is an easy ride. If some memories once had sharp-pointed edges, candidates for suppression, they were now worn down, the edges smoothed. Today, a more dispassionate view prevails.

Holding the books and reading the tiny handwriting from 1929 and 1930, I gain a greater insight of Nate. Reading the 1944 entries, I recall the times with this special uncle.

Yes, I visited for a week, but I stayed a lifetime!

December 2005

THE PATHFINDER

Exhibiting the determination that a sea-bound lemming would admire, the Toyota charged on, leaving pavement and gravel behind. It had used up a grassy lane, entered a pasture, passed an abandoned barn, topped a hill, and disappeared. David and Julia, following in their van, refused to go farther. The Toyota had suddenly dropped from view. David jumped out of the van and hurried to the crest of the hill, fearing the worst: a drop-off or a cliff, not visible to the Toyota's driver until too late. David's in-laws, Bill and Mary Heck, and the boys were in the car. Bill was the driver. The boys were Trevor and Hayden, David's and Julia's young sons.

The two vehicles had been traveling to the Heck's farm in Adams County, Ohio. En route the Toyota had taken an unplanned turn unto "Crooked Road", a township road not known to any of these visitors to the southern Ohio hills. As they left the State Route 247 behind, David knew young Trevor was responsible for this adventure.

Trevor, at an early age, had shown an interest in all types of thoroughfares. He seemed to think that streets, avenues, interstates, highways, and footpaths had been created just for him. He had a remarkable knack for recalling roads and their destinations after just once traveled. He seemed to have the goal of traveling every byway on the North American continent and this wavy line on the map called "Crooked Road" was one of them. The driver, Granddad "Poppy" Bill, compliant when it came to his grandson, agreed to the change in travel plans without informing David and Julia following in their van.

Trevor's parents first noticed his interest in things "road-related" when he was less than two. One of his first words was "bump"—a term he used for anything that disturbed the surface of pavement. When adjoining sections of sidewalk, influenced by Ohio's freeze/thaw weather, had decided to go separate ways, Trevor would stop on his walk, inspect the misalignment and announce it was a "bump." On one family-reunion picnic, when he was just into walking, he discovered two speed bumps on the nearby park road. Most of the day was spent going from one speed bump to the other, standing on them, and declaring for all that they were bumps. Adults and children were on the alert to run out and grab him when a car was entering or leaving the park.

His next phase, at two years of age, was sign-post shaking. There were sidewalks where he lived in Cincinnati. On each street corner there was a metal sign post with the street name mounted at the top. He never passed a sign without first stopping, looking up at it, grabbing, and shaking it. He knew which ones were the most susceptible to his effort—which name-bearing metal plate at the top would move the most.

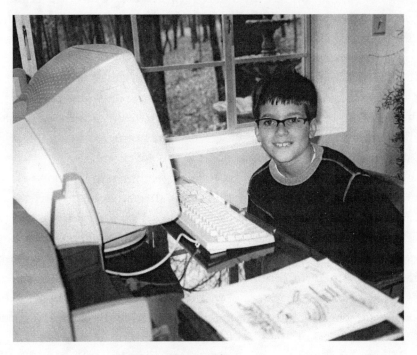

Trevor Sharp

At times he broadened his pole-shaking to something other than street signs. Once when traveling, the family stopped at a Burger King to get something to eat. The stop had been influenced by a very high sign that could easily be seen from the interstate. The sign, at least 80 feet high on a concrete pole, was next to the parking lot. Trevor was out of the car and hurried to the pole. Could it have been his first negative experience at pole shaking? He seemed puzzled. After eating, he returned to the pole and the sign. The result was the same–no movement at the top.

At four years old, a whole new world opened up for Trevor when he learned that those symbols on the street signs had meaning. It was then he began "reading" each one. When riding in the backseat of the car he would request the driver take different routes to their destinations and on the return home. It was not long before he knew the name for every street in his community and the best route for going to those places his family frequented.

Trevor became his mother's pathfinder when he accompanied her on errands and trips in the city. If he had been to a particular destination one time, he could recall the route taken and share that knowledge with those in the vehicle. One time Julia and he had to go to Union Terminal in downtown Cincinnati. Julia was unsure of the turns and exits. No problem. From the rear seat the pre-schooler took her through several turns in their community of Wyoming, onto Galbraith Road, to the interstate and told her which exit to take for Union Terminal. He nailed it.

However, Trevor was not infallible. Piling into the car, the family took a trip to David's relatives in Indiana. "Indiana" was a first for Trevor, a route not previously taken. The parents did not know the Pathfinder was mentally logging this new and exciting two hundred mile route. The next year (Trevor was five) the family took a trip to "Indiana" again except this time it was to Julia's relatives just across the border fifty miles away. On this trip Trevor kept telling his dad that this was not the way to Indiana. David and Julia could not think why Trevor was taking such an adamant stand. Then, they remembered. On the trip the previous year they must have kept referring to the state as the destination rather than the city of Lafayette.

Marynelle and I learned the Pathfinder could use this skill to his advantage at the expense of others. One day when we took Trevor and Hayden on an outing, it came time for lunch. Most of our morning activities had been of Trevor's choosing, so we gave Hayden the chance to pick our lunch destination. He wanted to go to Wendy's, Trevor wanted Burger King. Hayden does not share his brother's talent for routes and direction. He knew what he wanted but did not know how to get there. Neither did we, so we turned to the one in the car who could. Trevor took us on a meandering, wandering ride. "Here it is," he said. I looked up and it was a Burger King. He claimed that he had become confused. I knew better, looked at the disappointment in his brother's big eyes, and did some chewing out.

I had to be careful though because, obviously, we were at the mercy of the only one that could get us back home. We were captives in our own car.

Trevor was seven when he accompanied his mother for a ride across the Ohio River into Kentucky. They were going to Julia's brother's home. There are three bridge possibilities between Cincinnati and Northern Kentucky. Trevor knew the route and told his mother that they were taking the wrong bridge. They were not taking the right road. After some time Julia decided that he was right because the surroundings did not look familiar. She turned around in Kentucky and crossed the river back into Cincinnati.

Now, the Pathfinder from the back seat was in command. She took the bridge of Trevor's choosing to Kentucky. She took the turns in Kentucky he selected. They arrived at their destination in Fort Thomas. Julia had managed to turn a thirty-minute trip into an hour and half. For Trevor, it was a great adventure.

David, from the hilltop, looked down on a sea of grass waving in the summer breeze. The car was not to be seen. Could they have kept going? Wait! He caught a glimpse of something red in the tall foliage below. It was the Toyota's rooftop! It was as if some alien intruder had dropped out of the heavens and fouled a peaceful scene. The Toyota began to move in the grass as tall as its rooftop. David watched as Bill tried to turn the car around and drive back up the hill. It was of no use. The grade and the grass were too much for the car. The four passengers piled out and walked back up the hill leaving the car behind. "Trevor wanted us to take this road," Bill and Mary said. David, keeping his real thoughts to himself, said, "What road? This is a pasture."

They found a local farmer, who with his tractor and a chain, pulled them back up the hill. The farmer told them there had not been a road there for at least fifty years. One wonders how the tale of the Toyota going cross-country plays in the local community.

The Pathfinder learned a valuable lesson that day–maps were not infallible. Some become out-dated. This map was revised on the spot–"Crooked Road" was crossed out. In the future he wouldn't need a map, for this non-road had a special niche in the Pathfinder's memory bank.

January 2006

A FORTNIGHT IN GERMANY

"What did you like best about your trip to Germany?" You know the question is coming, but knowing doesn't make the answer any easier. That's because the visit has been a panorama of images, ones that will dim with time, but today are still vivid.

There was Innsbruck nestled in its valley embraced by the Austrian Alps. There was the cathedral in Ulm and the university city of Heidelberg with its medieval castle on the scenic Neckar River. The resort of Garmisch in the German Alps contrasted to the bustle and sophistication of Stuttgart. And of course there was the spa city of Baden-Baden.

The towns of scenic Mittenwald and charming Altensteig with its winding, switchback streets and quaint Christmas market will remain in my reverie for some time.

The visit included the castles at Neuschwanstein and Hohenzollern. It was a tour of Christmas markets, from the commercial ones of the cities to the booths of local organizations in the markets of the smaller towns. The women shopped–the men calorie-loaded: *Wurst, Flammkuchen, Kartoffelu Kuchen,* and *Bier.* It was two weeks of sights, fun, and togetherness with a Germanic backdrop.

One of the best memories is of the leisurely walks near Althengstett, where Marynelle's son Ben, and his wife, Marion, live. Their home is near the edge of town. A right turn, a left turn and a jaunt of three hundred meters brings you to the start of a country trail for walking and biking. It is also used by farmers for moving powered farm machinery between fields.

One can take this trail on a circuitous route in the country and end up back at a different point in Althengstett than where you started. The trail is paved except for a short stretch. And that stretch looks like a country lane from boyhood–two wheel-worn tracks with a grass strip between them. Altogether the trail is probably 2 1/2 kilometers in length–just right for old legs and an old dog. *Spaetzle*, which means noodle, led the way, a taut leash at all times unless a scent required a brief pause.

It must be the "country" in me, for pastoral scenes rank high on my list. The trail provides all of that and distant views as well. The trail starts on a gradual climb on a hillside. The hill is topped with a large woods which is never entered by the trail but always stays to the right as the trail makes its climb. On the left and down the hill is a picturesque small valley with apple and plum orchards, green fields, and a few fields that have been plowed to lie fallow through the winter. There are some sheds in the orchards and a large barn near the valley's floor. And yes, the ever present, neatly stacked woodpiles on either side of the walk.

The Walk Home

It looks as if all woodpiles in Germany have been cut by the same Giant (after all this is the land of fairy tales.) All kindling is the same length and split to the same sizes. Is there some law that requires this? Is it a tradition and one is ostracized if they don't comply? Did the wood choppers of the country come together and set a standard?

Or, did the stove manufacturers specify the size of fire bowls and grates, thereby dictating the length of the kindling?

When you view the green fields in the valley you think it is spring. But a glance at the leafless fruit trees tells you that winter is close at hand. The fields are the last to give in to the coming season.

Not long into the walk the trail's highest point is reached. It is here we are close to the woods. Through the trees a house can be seen. It looks a bit sinister. You just know the wolf is in Grandmother's bed.

A trail for farm equipment comes in on the left from the farm below. The walking trail begins a gradual descent, hedges come alongside, and the woods are left behind. The valley to the northeast opens to view. A series of villages nestle there until the valley ascends between hills and disappears. The dark outline of The Black Forest is on the hills to the left and the hills to the right feature small fields and orchards. The road between Calw and Althengstett lies below.

To the west, five kilometers away, is a darkened, almost black, chasm-like slice. Down this tree-covered cut is the city of Calw, out of sight below. As the trail continues, hedges thick enough for birds and small animals to survive the winter appear. Fruit trees, evenly spaced, line the path. Some are mature and others newly planted. The trail has left the woods far behind and has turned in the direction of town.

Spaetzle steps up her pace as we near home. The exercise provided by the walk, the serenity of the scene, and the muted country sounds are therapy for the soul. The analyst's couch is not needed. Spaetzle's waggling tail suggests the same.

April 2006

OUTSOURCE IT!!

Yesterday I stopped over at the internet café for a cup of joe and some net surfing. As I looked around for a seat and a computer I spotted Cedric. I hadn't seen him for over a year so thought I might take a moment to catch up. Thinking it would take five minutes, Cedric's life not being very exciting, I asked how he was doing. Usually he was in a "woe is me" mode, never cheery, and expecting the worst.

He caught me off-guard when he said, "Man, everything's cool. Life's a warm fuzzy."

"Hey Ced, that's great to hear, what gives?"

"I'm going down the aisle, man–tying the knot, pooling debts."

"Wow!!" I had never known him to have any kind of a relationship with the opposite sex, platonic or otherwise. Stunned, I managed to mumble a "–gratulations and who's the lucky girl?"

"Her name is Imogene and she's awesome, a real fox."

"Does she live around here?"

"Nah, she lives in Cleveland."

"Nebraska?" I asked.

"Man, no, the big one, in Ohio!"

Knowing Cedric tended to be reclusive, having never left the state in his 38 years, and knowing Cleveland was nine hundred miles away, I asked, "How did you ever meet someone from Ohio?"

"In a chat-room, man, on the internet, right in this room."

"That's great. I know of several successful couplings using the old net. And when did Mr. Romeo sitting here in front of me, pop the question?" I asked.

"I haven't and I'm not going to," was the surprising response.

Now, how can two people tie the knot and one of them not know they are being tied? There had been so much in the news lately about people in hospital beds not being fully with it. Could she be comatose, not really aware? Who would perform such a ceremony? Hesitantly, I pursued the subject.

"Cedric, you're getting married and the woman knows nothing about this minor little event in her life?"

"She will soon; I'm having a guy propose for me this weekend in Cleveland, right after the Indians game on Saturday."

"Oh, does she have season tickets?"

"Nah, she sells beer at the Indians' games, she doesn't like baseball. She's a Browns' fan, they tip better."

"Wait a minute. Did you say someone else is going to propose for you? Isn't that a little impersonal for such a personal moment in one's life?"

"You know how I wig out when I travel–those panic attacks. So, I decided to contract out my proposal, have someone do it for me."

"But you can't do that–and who in their right mind would undertake such a task? And if you haven't gone to Cleveland, does this mean you haven't met her?"

"Chill out Dude. The old 'net's a cool tool," said Cedric, "A great way to meet people and not get off your rear end. Classy chicks like Imogene. And you can find all kinds of services on the net, like a "marriage proposal service" which charges a mere twenty-five dollars. You just can't beat it."

"Cedric, a marriage proposal is something the woman never forgets. She remembers where you proposed, how you fumbled with the miniscule diamond you're making payments on, the weather, and how romantic it was when you mumbled," 'Two can live as cheaply as one.' "Those are precious memories that are relived when the faded VCR tape is shown the grandkids. That's something you will never experience if you insist on continuing with this charade of a romance."

"Man, where have you been? You're passe," said Cedric. "Don't you know about contracting out, outsourcing jobs, those boring jobs you don't want to do? That's all I'm doing–outsourcing a job to a specialist that has specific skills in a particular area. Every cat in the country is outsourcing or being outsourced and I don't plan to be left out."

"What do you mean?"

"Why this is just another thing our great country leads the world in."

"You mean contracting out?"

"Certainly, it's in the very fabric of our lives. It's all around us."

"Like what?" I insisted.

"Like that SUV you drive. Very few of the parts are made by GM. Those cats outsource them to the cheapest back alley producer they can find."

"Well, I know that," I said. "That's been going on for years. That's Detroit for you. They're not representative of what this great country is about."

"No way," said Cedric. "They're even outsourcing social services. States and local governments are doing less and contractors more for the most needy, those physically and mentally challenged. I know, there are stories everyday in the news about the lousy service some contractors provide. But, they seem to get away with it. And you know as well as I, we can't have those overpaid state employees and their benefits doing the job anymore."

Cedric continued, "How about those clothes you are wearing that were bought at Wal-Mart? They were outsourced by the company whose label is on your shirt–some sweat shop in Thailand, probably. I know, there are child labor stories and all that, but at least those people have jobs. It's too bad people in South Carolina that used to make the clothes don't have jobs. But, let me assure you, the outsourcing of my marriage proposal causes no job loss."

He was on a roll, "Do you know that some married couples even out-source having their baby to a surrogate mother? And how about Iraq?"

Immediately I became defensive. "What about Iraq?"

"It's contracted out, too."

"I don't call those Marines and army troops outsourcing," I said.

" Not them. The companies that are restoring the infrastructure or at least contracted to do it, like Halliburton. Some companies are even contracted to conduct military activities, you know, shoot people. And they are getting a lot more bucks to shoot than our poor soldiers get. That's real outsourcing of your job if you ask me. If they can do that why can't I outsource something beautiful, like my proposal?"

Cedric couldn't be stopped. He continued, "Some states are letting contractors run public schools. The jury is still out on that one, you know, those mandated tests and all. And man, I was fired when my computer job went to India. If those cats in Bombay can figure out the squirreled-up software we sent them to service, more power to them. We sure couldn't figure it out."

"Like so many new concepts, this, too, will run its course," I said.

"No way, the surface has only been scratched of using this wonderful tool to fuel our economy. Why, do you know that huge dairy farm over in Cargill County?"

"Yes," I said, for I had just passed it last week.

"Well, those six hundred and fifty cows over there are producing more than just milk." Cedric replied.

"Like what?"

"A cow eats eighteen hours out of a twenty-four hour day. That sweet-smelling clover going in the front end comes out in an entirely different condition once the cow is through with it. And removal of that product is outsourced by the dairy to an independent contractor. A dairy farmer is after one thing—milk production. They can't be bothered with all that crap so they turn to a company with manure expertise."

"What would anyone want with the loads of manure that would come from six hundred and fifty cows?" I asked.

"Well, the company is hauling it out to their place, piling it up, sticking pipes down in it and capturing methane gas for energy use." I'd never heard of such a thing and asked the location of the manure pile so that I might go see it.

"Oh, it's out by the big wind turbines over by Odorville," Cedric replied.

"Wind turbines and methane. I guess they are into energy alternatives in a big way."

"No, manure is their only interest—the wind turbines are just there to blow the horrible stink over into the next county."

Cedric was wearing me down. I couldn't stop him, "You heard about that new automobile company that started up last year down in Kentucky?"

I had, but knew little about the hare-brained idea to start up a new automobile company when existing manufacturers were dropping models and sales were down.

"They have become the darling of the outsourcing world," said Cedric.

"How do you mean?"

"They have only twelve people working at the company; they do nothing except write contracts. They manufacture not one thing, yet, they sold four hundred and fifty thousand cars last year."

"What about those things that must be done to produce and sell a car, like design, engineering, production, and marketing?"

"All outsourced to others. However, the twelve employees do have a special skill. They are all linguists since all the outsourcing is off-shore. They have people who can speak Czech, Chinese, Korean, Japanese, Thai, all kinds of languages. If the Iraqi mess gets resolved they plan to contract with them as well."

I was incredulous. "You have to be joking, not an Iraqi!"

"No I'm not joking. Those Kentuckians have just hired Sadam Hussein's barber for the Arabic spot on the staff."

Cedric arose from his seat and motioned for me to sit down at the computer. "I've got to go now, but listen man, you need to get on board and ride this outsourcing wave into the future."

He waved good-by as he headed toward the door. Suddenly, he turned and hollered across the room, "Hey, Dude, how about being my best man?"

"Nah," I said, "OUTSOURCE IT!!"

September 2006

BOYHOOD'S NORTHWEST PASSAGE

OR

A PLACE TO WADE

Boys and water go together. Not the water in the bathtub awaiting the dirt-streaked body, or the water to wet the toothbrush at the end of the day. Those are waters to be avoided, waters that have no useful purpose as seen by a boy. Boys want water to wade in, float sticks, skip stones, build dams, catch crawdads.

A boy's interest in water can be seen at an early age. One can observe a little tot, in his very best clothes, with his very best shoes, headed to church with his family. It is a beautiful April day after an early morning shower, when a parking lot puddle catches his eye. He heads straight for the shower-deposited gift with absolutely no thought given to his shiny footwear and plunges in. No amount of pleading or threats can deter him from his course. For him it is a spiritual moment. It is his "going to church."

Doug Tron and I, as young boys, played together a lot, particularly in the summer. My mother contended that during the summer we would play together two days, fight the third, stay home on the fourth day, and on the fifth day start the cycle over. We had a wide range of activities: shooting baskets and guns, building tree houses, hiking to the woods, sleeping in a cabin in the woods, and hurrying home to eat breakfast the next morning. Unfortunately, we lived where no water of any significance was within range of our tiny bikes and legs to pump them. There were no lakes or streams of any size nearby. We lived in the flat Ohio countryside where streams started, too immature to even be given names; streams that might not exist unless there had been some recent rainfall.

One of the places to play in water was a nearby ditch that had been dug for drainage of area farmland. Farmers paid taxes based on the acres they possessed that drained into the ditch. For us it was a

94

place to get muddy and catch crawdads. Its flow was dependent on rainfall, never containing enough for a swim or a wade to the knees. Our parents never worried about us around the ditch. To drown, one would have had to stand on his head in the ditch, something neither of us could do.

We were persistent in our search for water. One time Doug discovered a new water hole. It was along the Erie tracks on the side that drained toward the Gulf of Mexico. It was the Erie locomotives going west that one would hear while lying in bed at night.

Doug Tron and Ned Sharp

Two longs, a short and a long at the Espyville crossing to be followed by the same whistle warning at the crossing near Eisele's farm. When in grade school, it was the steam whistle we heard; to be replaced by the diesel's horn when we were in high school. The water hole by the tracks was not far from the Eisele crossing. We ventured there only a few times because of its small size and it being a repository for what engines and freight cars would discard as they passed.

One day Dad told me that the water on our farm drained toward the Gulf of St. Lawrence and the Atlantic, while the water on the other side of the Erie drained toward the Gulf of Mexico. I was amazed he would know this. He explained that the nearby ditch draining our acreage emptied into the Tymotchee Creek. The Tymotchee went into the Sandusky River, to Lake Erie, to the Niagara River, to Lake Ontario, to the St. Lawrence River, and finally to the Atlantic. This became clear after poring over the atlas. Our "continental divide" was the Erie Railroad and its dual tracks.

The Tron's farm was about one third of a mile from ours. The barns were visible between the two. One of our little experiments was to set up a signaling system between us by draping a cloth out the windows of the barns. A cloth appearing out the window would indicate "come down and play." This system was short-lived because one had to climb up to see the other's signal or to send a signal. However, it was that signal which led me to go to Doug's house for some exploration and a "great discovery."

We spent a lot of time in the fields and woods of nearby farms and knew the area well. One day we ventured onto a new farm, unsure of exactly where we were or whose farm it was. We discovered a small pond. Small, but the largest single body of water we had ever found. We returned to the pond often, particularly in the spring when frogs were abundant and tadpoles were about. One warm spring-like day in February we could not resist. Clothes were hung on a tree limb and we waded in up to our waists. We were in February water that had been January ice. We had a "discussion" on the effects freezing water has on the human torso, as we turned blue.

We had a swale through our farm which carried water when there were heavy downpours. That was a real treat. If you hurried out right after the cloudburst and lightning moved away, there would be a fast-moving regular Colorado River right in the field closest to the house. I would jump in never considering that this water had run through a neighbor's pasture for horses, cows, and pigs. Maybe E-coli didn't exist then. Could it be a boy's immune system is extra vigilant?

As we grew older our bikes grew bigger, legs stronger, and our range of water exploration increased. By going four or five miles south we could reach the Scioto River, which was the main waterway in our school district. In the dry season the Scioto's brown flow was so slow you couldn't see it move. A stick thrown in would be there an hour later. If rainfall was heavy, the Scioto would leave its banks and flood all the low-lying farms near it. Often, we missed school because of the Scioto's closing roads. Buses were not permitted to go on any road covered with water, no matter its depth.

Rush Creek was a mile south of the Scioto. The creek came close to the road and on it was a dam. Our most fanciful dreams were answered for behind the dam was a pool of water adequate for dog paddling. We made several visits to this creek on our bikes making sure our mothers knew where we going. Our stays there plus the ride home could make for a long day.

About two miles farther south from the Rush Creek dam was a small quarry which we visited a few times. Here we could swim; however, the risks increased because of the water depth and size of the pool. It was a bike ride too long for me to undertake more than a few times.

Gradually, as we grew older we depended less on the water near home for pleasure and play. Occasionally, our mothers would take us to swim in Marion at a private quarry. It was very large with a portion of it roped off for waders and swimmers. The water was beautiful, clear, and blue, a delight to swim in. Later, Marion built a municipal pool, but we were long gone from the local scene by that time. It was never part of our water adventures.

Recently, I was on a hike in a woods with my wife, children, and grandchildren. There were some small streams coursing through the woods and over rocks. It was not long before the grandchildren and I were building dams, backing up the water, watching it seek new ways around the obstacles. We all became a bit wet and muddy. For me, it was a wonderful day. I had a flashback!

What do you suppose Doug Tron is doing today?

October 2006

HENRY–WHO'S YOUR DADDY???

My liking of history, particularly of the United States, has engendered my interest in genealogy. When events of historical significance occurred, were my ancestors involved or affected? What drove them to migrate around 1800 from the Atlantic states into the wilds of Ohio, Kentucky, and Tennessee; some staying for a generation or two, then moving to land beyond the Mississippi?

I'm not a purist in the search for ancestors. I don't always get the proof genealogists require to verify lineage: evidence such as birth certificates, bible records, census data, obituaries, and such. I sometimes accept another searcher's assertion as factual and don't request supporting data. If I am told that Great Aunt Hilda ran off with the hired man, I don't ask for proof, but accept it. This is risky if I spend much time with a true genealogist who requires verifiable evidence.

I was into genealogy very early in life. I didn't know that was what it was called when I asked family questions and listened to uncles' tales. I wasn't recording facts or the relative's yarns (many highly inaccurate), but enough was remembered to provide the basis for deeper research later. That experience has provided much pleasure and many puzzles. The search can be never-ending–there will always be dead-ends.

My dead-end is Henry. Henry (1784 to 1856) is in my line, five generations back. He is my Great-Great-Great-Grandfather Sharp. In over 25 years of a somewhat less than organized search, I've never been able to determine his parents.

My father knew some stories about our ancestors but he never mentioned a Henry.

It was a few years after Dad died in 1978 that I ran across a Union County (Ohio) history that had a biographical sketch of a Robert Sharp (1810 to 1892). Among other things it listed his children (including my Great-Grandfather Russell), his wives (two) and, most importantly, his parents. They were Henry Sharp and Nancy Trevillian, born in Albemarle County, Virginia. Henry went to Ohio sometime after 1800. He and Nancy married in 1809 in Ross County, Ohio.

A large portion of Ohio had been set aside as Virginia Military Lands for Revolutionary War veterans. As a result, much of southern Ohio was settled by Virginians. Henry settled on a land patent in the military lands. However, he was not a veteran nor is it known who had the original warrant for the land. Henry remained on the land until his death.

I had known for some years that there was a Robert Sharp and a Robert Sharp, Jr. who lived in Albemarle County in the late 1700s and early 1800s. I knew the latter had served as a captain in the war. Both were the right age to have been Henry's father, but my research had never been able to find any link between Henry and the Roberts. Henry had named his first son (my great-great-grandfather) Robert. Naming a first son after one of the boy's grandfathers was a tradition among the English and Scotch-Irish. However, a naming tradition fell short of the required evidence for lineage.

So, I don't know Henry's parents and grandparents, my sixth and seventh generations back. However, I do know possibly the eighth through the tenth generation. I know this because of another's research and DNA testing.

One Sharp researcher (Al Sharp) has scoured the records of early Virginia and verified his ancestry back to William Sharpe. William arrived at Jamestown in 1620. William lived from 1585 to 1630 and was a member of the House of Burgesses. Al Sharp, being a persistent and thorough genealogist had his DNA determined. Al contacted me to have my DNA checked. Bingo! My thirty-seven markers were identical to Al's. My trail, too, goes back to Old William. Now, my task is to find the generations between Henry and Old William.

Knowing all this is a big breakthrough. Yet, I feel responsible for Henry. I can't just move on to the other surnames on my tree: Sheltons, Yearsleys, and Rittenhouses. I can't leave Henry out in the cold. I must find his genealogical links back to Old William of Jamestown. I can't abandon him.

HENRY — WHO'S YOUR DADDY???

December 2006

99

Resources:
Henry Howe, "Union County History of 1883" Ohio
Sharpe/Sharp DNA Testing Project, FamilyTreeDNA.com

CREEPER

Have you ever, when alone, known darn well that you aren't? The one place I should be able to be alone with my thoughts is my computer room/den/library/nap-site. There have been signs for some time that something else resides in my retreat.

It isn't some eerie ghost-like presence that has invaded my domain; well, maybe sort of eerie but it doesn't moan or rattle chains. It is five and one-half feet long, four feet wide and one quarter inch tall. It is multi-colored, with red dominating, and it must have been designed by someone not doing well in rehab. I can live with all that; after all it was a gift. Colors are not a big deal since I'm nearly color-blind. Its design only bothers me when I happen to forget and look its way.

Creeper is the little rug in front of my couch. I have used up enough years now to appreciate the significant role a couch plays in my well-being. I view my couch as a veritable temple. In my little room it is not there to sit on and watch TV. It has one function—naps. And the key to good nap-taking is a room where all objects co-exist harmoniously. Clutter included.

But, there appears to be an issue between the rug and the couch. The rug's place is in front of the couch on the carpeted floor. The rug moves and I don't know why. Oh, it doesn't jump up and down or run sprints, but it does move. Have you ever watched a clock on the wall to see if you could see movement in the big hand? Of course you have; you went to school didn't you? We've all wished for recess to come. You could never see that big hand move, but it did.

The rug is like that big hand. I have sat and stared at that red design until nauseated and seen absolutely nothing. Leave the room for a couple of hours, come back, and the rug has moved. Stay away for a day, walk in, and it has moved. At times it seems more active than others. It seems to be trying to get away from the couch or possibly it is being drawn to a footstool in whose direction it tends to move.

Could there be something to do with physics that influences Creeper? I didn't do so well in physics in high school. I do know where the sun rises and the ol' earth is spinning eastward to cause that, but Creeper fights that eastward spin and always goes toward the southwest, toward the footstool and away from the couch. Why is that? Can a footstool have hidden powers? There have been times when returning from vacation I have found Creeper has reached the footstool and developed folds as it pushes against its legs. My mind drifts: could the rug have a crush on the footstool, but the footstool has other interests?

Actually, I'm coming around to that spirit-world thing. I believe Creeper is infected with a spirit.

Wait! That's it! It's *The Sign*! I should have known. *The Sign* always shows up every four years during presidential campaigns. It likes to make predictions about the outcome of the election. And it is infallible. Well, almost. There was that time it predicted Ross Perot in a landslide.

The Sign is using Creeper to deliver a prediction! This is unheard of. Normally, *The Sign* uses cigarette smoke rings to bring its message. Apparently, the banning of smoking in public places has forced *The Sign* to turn elsewhere for its parasitic journey.

Let's see, Creeper has been moving in a southwestwardly direction. It has to be–that's it, John McCain! Arizona is in that direction. You can't get much more southwest from Lincoln than Arizona. But as I focus on Creeper, McCain just doesn't resonate.

Peering deeply into that ugly rug *The Sign's* message becomes much clearer. There is no mistake. There is another candidate out there to the southwest.

The Sign is saying, "Think Taos man, come on Bunky, think pueblos, it's New Mexico. Bunky, Governor Bill Richardson will be the next President of The United States."

Creeper, caught up in the moment, fired a plea, "Hey Bunky, when you're in Vegas, put a hundred down on the Gov for me!"

February 2007

HOMECOMING

Trevor Petersen's first homecoming was an unforgettable family celebration.

Dave and Kelli had decided to adopt a child. They had investigated the highly reputable Holt International Children's Services. They liked what they found, Holt seemed a good fit, and was chosen by them to start the adoption process.

Holt Services has extensive experience in overseas adoptions, particularly in Asia. Dave and Kelli knew from the outset that their baby would be from Korea. Kelli, whose profession is in Human Resources, found the Holt background check of Dave and her far exceeded any job application she had seen. It was a detailed screening by the agency to assure a loving, nurturing home awaited the child.

The process started in February 1998. In September, they learned they would be getting a baby boy, born on June 12, the same birthday as Kelli's father, Gordon. It was a good omen. Gordon, who had served in the Korean War, had passed away in 1995.

Finally, Dave and Kelli received word the baby would be arriving at the Des Moines airport November 24, 1998. It had been nine long months. They selected the name Trevor.

Three babies were to arrive from Seoul, each accompanied by a Korean woman that cared for them on the flight. Family members and friends were gathered in the passenger lounge area, something permitted before security restrictions resulting from 9/11 were imposed. Dave and Kelli wanted a quiet, unobtrusive welcoming for Trevor. However, grandparents, aunts, uncles, and cousins from Nebraska and Iowa awaited the plane.

The anticipation increased as the plane was not on time. But soon we heard that it was on the ground and headed for the gate.

Passengers from the plane trickled through the door to the lounge. It seemed they would never stop coming. Where were the babies? Many passengers smiled at the anxiously awaiting crowd, and one woman passenger announced to all, "They are on the plane!"

Finally, a Holt representative left the lounge and entered the plane. The new parents moved closer to the door. It was then the babies appeared at the entrance, each in the arms of their Korean caregivers. The Holt representative led the women and the bundled babies to the waiting parents. Each of the babies was handed to an anxious mother.

The bright-eyed, alert boy was given to Kelli. She extended her arms to look at him. Trevor checked her out as well. Trevor touched Kelli's cheek with an open mouth and then his tiny hand fingered

Dave, Kelli, and Trevor Petersen

her shiny earring. It was a beautiful moment and beginning for this new family of three.

The family entourage in the airport lounge celebrated Trevor's homecoming. Each held the baby for a few moments, Trevor never protesting. It was as if the newly arrived children and their families were wrapped in an aura of love and caring. The airport lounge was hosting a love-fest!

Today, Trevor Petersen is nine years old. His family celebrates his homecoming arrival each November 24. He is a remarkable boy with exceptional agility, both mental and physical. He has an abounding curiosity and is an excellent student.

I've attended several homecoming events over the years. Many have involved a football game. I don't remember the specifics of any of them. But, I will never forget the Des Moines homecoming when that tiny baby boy entered into his mother's arms—and all our lives.

May 2007

1918 INFLUENZA

We begin to hear and read of influenza outbreaks in different parts of the world each autumn. Asia seems to be the incubator for many of these events. A few years ago it was SARS; just last winter we were being warned of the bird flu strain H5N1. Fortunately, neither developed into world-wide threats; both were confined to specific localities.

Such was not the case of the great flu pandemic which circled the globe in 1918. It hit particularly hard in the United States beginning in the spring. In September twelve thousand Americans died and in October the number jumped to one hundred ninety-five thousand. During seventeen horrifying months, before the disease had run its course, it is estimated twenty-five million Americans were sickened and six hundred seventy thousand died. The number of deaths exceeded the total of all the 20th century wars in which Americans fought. It was the worst epidemic in American history.

The epidemic in the United States was interwoven with the wave of patriotism that swept the country in response to our entering the war in Europe. Rallies and bond drives, resulting in congregating crowds, gave the disease ideal conditions for spreading among the population. Also, those entering the armed services were housed in camps that provided the virus the necessary fuel to rage virtually unchecked. During influenza outbreaks the young and elderly are normally the most vulnerable. This was not the case in 1918. The greatest number of deaths were of those between fifteen and forty years of age. It took the most robust, those in the prime of life. Death was quick, terrible, and terrifying.

I don't recall my school history books covering this event. They may have, but for me it wasn't necessary. As a boy I heard the stories told by my mother and her siblings; stories of fear and heartbreak over family losses caused by the frightening disease.

My mother's family lived in Broadway, Ohio, a small village in Union County. In 1918, the two youngest of the family were Mom (Ferne) and Edith, nine and six years of age. There were eight older siblings. In 1913, Dode, an older brother, married a pretty local girl, Josephine Knox. Dode was twenty and Josephine was eighteen. The first child, Lavon, arrived in 1916, and Hubert was born in 1918. Josephine was one of those stricken in the October surge of flu cases. Tragically, Josephine died leaving the children motherless. With the help of relatives, particularly older siblings, Lavon was able to stay with her father, Dode.

Josephine Knox Shelton

Hubert went to stay with Dode's brother and wife. Ultimately, Hubert was adopted by Dwight and Zell Shelton.

The wave of patriotism and the drive to defeat the *Kaiser* swept the country in 1918. Caught up in that wave was one of the brothers. Paul went into the army September 12, 1918. He was sent to Camp Sherman at Chillicothe, Ohio. Camp Sherman was constructed for training of recruits. The camp housed over forty thousand soldiers, ideal conditions for the influenza's spread. In September there were one thousand four hundred cases reported at the camp. That number quadrupled to over five thousand six hundred the next month. Nearly twelve hundred soldiers died.

Paul's mother, Estella Shelton, rushed to Camp Sherman to assist in caring for the sick. Being small in stature she became known as "Little

Mother" by those she tended. Paul had become one of the ill. On October 12, 1918 Paul died, five weeks after entering the service. He was twenty-one. He was brought home to be buried in the Broadway cemetery, a graveyard shared with many Sheltons.

Estella returned from Camp Sherman exhausted and then she, too, became ill. She died Christmas Day, 1918. My mother's recollection of that day is that Edith and she were carried next door to the neighbors. Her lone Christmas gift was an orange.

Estella Yearsley Shelton

Estella's death was a particularly devastating event for the family. She was the rock on whom the children depended and the glue that held them together. Five children were still at home: Nate, Sewell, John, Ferne, and Edith.

Nate helped provide a home for the two younger boys. Ferne and Edith were raised by an older sister, Esther, and her husband, Harry Hershberger. Harry and Esther were quite young and newly married, when they took the girls. A strong bond among the three sisters existed to the end. Although Esther was just a few years older than the two girls she was the "mother" and anchor they so desperately needed.

The dreaded disease began to ebb in the early months of 1919. The deaths became fewer and the boys began returning home from the Great War.

The country's limited role in the war, compared to Britain and France, was glorified in history annals. However, the great swath the epidemic cut through the population was accorded little comment by those same historians.

October 2007

Resources:
Lynette Iezzoni, *Influenza 1918* (New York: TV Books, L.L.C.)
National Park Service History/Archeology

THE RELIABLES

It has been fifteen years since I have worked in an office environment. In those fifteen years I have met many retirees that worked in similar situations as I. Listening to some of their stories, I have decided we shared many of the same experiences, though the industry or service in which we toiled may have been quite different. One activity that we all experienced was changes to the organization. Some called them upheavals.

Systemic problems could be isolated and solutions proposed; but, if the solutions were computer systems-dependent, an unacceptable timeline would result. Instead of changing the system, an attack on the organizational structure would be made. One fascinating aspect of every organization overhaul would be personnel assignments; where would we end up, who would our boss be, would our work assignment change? It was a study in human nature to observe how people would react to workplace changes. However, there were a few that would be oblivious to the reorganizing cyclone about them, for they would never change, no matter their destiny in the new alignment. They had their routine down and were not interested in taking on a new role. They were reliable. Reliable in the sense that they would continue to do as before, maintain the status quo, hunker down, and let others contend with the changes.

It seems my fellow retirees had similar experiences and the same "reliable" characters existed in those experiences. We shared stories of *The Reliables.*

Mosely was fairly effective in his job. The problem was that he was never there to demonstrate that effectiveness. He was a hypochondriac. He could be triggered to go into his death march with the most innocent of suggestions. If someone sneezed in the office before lunch, Mosely would be catching a cold and have to depart by 2:00 p.m. to go home to his bed. Flu was a popular malady for him, one that could cause a prolonged hiatus under his favorite quilt. The men in the office, having little empathy for Mosely's mania, would feign stomach aches, headaches, backaches, and every other kind of ache covered in medical school. They would see how long Mosely would go before having a similar complaint and ultimately go home to die. His peers would set up a betting pool as to when departure would occur. Fortunately, Mosely never worked near a pregnant woman. If he had, and the mother-to-be showed signs of discomfort, Mosely would have rushed home to give birth. You could rely on it!

Elwood was the nomad of the workplace, never staying long in one office, and the first to be offered up in a reorganization. Someone, forsaking wisdom, in the distant past, had promoted Elwood to a supervisory position. As a result, he commanded a supervisory position no matter where the reorganization would plop him. Neither his new work force nor his superior jumped with joy when Elwood arrived at his new assignment. Elwood was part of the "clean desk" fraternity, a group that led one to believe they had a subversive agenda. Nothing ever was seen on the top of Elwood's desk. Reports, studies, correspondence coming in, or going out would land on his desk and without shutting off their engines take off and fly elsewhere. Elwood never read anything produced by his office, but depended totally on his people to defend their product. The quality and accuracy of their work was never assessed by him. What he found important was that all "due dates" were met. Elwood reliably met all "due dates."

One of my co-workers had an adage that went something like this, "Unattended, man will do what he likes, regardless of its need or usefulness."

Wheatley and Faulkner fulfilled this adage.

Wheatley would be sucked up into the whirling vortex of the organizational realignment and be spit out into the realm of some unsuspecting middle manager. He led the pack in jobs held. Over the years he had honed his skills at being a gofer. Wheatley would report to his new supervisor who would assign him to some special project. The tasking would never stick with Wheatley, for he would revert to his gofer role, once his supervisor turned his attention elsewhere.

Coordination among offices was required on many tasks. Wheatley excelled at carrying a report, produced by his office, for coordination by others. His boss would say, "Wheatley, we need Carmichael's sign-off on this. Go down to his office and get it now. This was due out two years ago." Wheatley would navigate the maze of corridors, halls, and offices; a maze no self-respecting laboratory rat would undertake. Upon arriving at Carmichael's alcove, Wheatley would stand by awaiting the much desired signature. If Carmichael had questions about the report, Wheatley was of no help–he had no clue about the contents of the report, had no intention of reading it, and wouldn't have understood it if he did. He was smart, just not interested. He spent his career in the corridors carrying something, somewhere.

Faulkner was a supervisor over about twenty-five people. His quirk was shopping and getting the best bargain in doing so. This meant if you worked for Faulkner you became a shopper as well–for him that is! His employees traveled a great deal. He knew where they were going and what the best bargains were in the area to be traveled. The people who worked for him were responsible for the curio-filled cabinets in which he and his wife gloried. Avoiding Faulkner right before departing on the plane was impossible. He would approach the traveler with a shopping list. If you expected words of wisdom about the task, maybe even some guidance before departing, forget it. A shopping list, yes. You could rely on Faulkner.

Today, I'm no longer concerned with organizational changes. Well, that's not really true. Just yesterday Marynelle told me to organize my workbench or she would put "all that junk" in her garage sale this coming week-end.

I'm going to pull a "Mosely" on her and get under my quilt.

November 2007

TO OL' VIRGINNY

Part One

Pressure was mounting. Marynelle had a free airline ticket that had to be used by the end of June. It was now the first of May and I had not been attentive to her pleas that I help her select a destination. Memorial weekend was approaching; we had had a memorable such weekend nine years ago in Washington D.C.–she thought it time to return. George W. Bush would be on his ranch, Congress would be home, the lobbyists would be out of town, and the government employees would be gone on a holiday respite. It would be a good time to tour, attend the concert on the Capitol's lawn, and watch the Memorial Day parade.

I was not as gung-ho as she about returning to Washington. I had been stationed nearby when in the Army, had been to the Pentagon several times when working for the Air Force, and had visited four times as a tourist. However, I had been wanting to get down to Charlottesville and Afton in Virginia to pursue some genealogy/family related activities. Marynelle thought we could do both. So, it became a win-win trip–she got D.C. and I, down-state Virginia.

After landing at National, we picked up a rental car and headed south on I-95. And the rest of the world joined us! It was stop and go all the way to our exit at Fredericksburg.

Food became an obsession as we crawled down the interstate. The eight peanuts served on the plane had long since gone where peanuts go after five hours. We had visions of finding some down-home cooking along our route to Charlottesville. But exiting I-95 we entered the world of McDonalds and its kin, strip malls, gas stations, major shopping malls, etc. Where was the Virginia I remembered? We settled on Chilis, its menu a clone of ours in Lincoln.

After eating, we finally broke away from the exit's commercial clutter and entered the scenic countryside. There were many wooded areas adjoining the pastures and hayfields to form a rural checkerboard. The fields were fenced and small, unlike the large open fields of corn and soybeans in Nebraska. The roads were influenced by the contours of the countryside. Sometimes they would go over the hills and at other times around the hills. It made for a picturesque evening ride before sundown.

There were two reasons for my wanting to get down into central Virginia and out to the Blue Ridge. I had learned that a Robert Sharp Jr. had built a house in 1794 on an Albemarle County farm. The house was on the Limestone Farm and it was there Al Sharp was to meet us the next morning. Al was a genealogist with a particular interest in identifying the Sharps in early Virginia. Al and I had been speculating that Robert Sharp Jr. was in my direct genealogical line. Proof was lacking.

The second reason for our trip was out on the eastern slope of the Blue Ridge. I knew of several distant cousins near Afton. Since Limestone Farm was only an hour away from where several of them lived, I wanted to take this opportunity to finally meet them.

We had time before dark to go to Shadwell to locate the farm. We wanted to find it so that the next day's rendezvous with Al Sharp would not be hampered by a lengthy search for it. We found the entrance to the farm's lane as the sun was setting. We were excited about what lie ahead the next day. Marynelle and I were particularly excited that the farm was so close to Shadwell, the birthplace of Thomas Jefferson.

The next morning we headed out of Charlottesville the wrong way and before we reversed our course we had eaten up thirty minutes of drive-time. I was concerned Al might be gone, but as we drove up to the gate there was another car there. We saw a man walking through the field on the right toward the gate. Marynelle and I introduced ourselves to Al.

Mr. Johnson, the current owner of the property, arrived to unlock the gate and let us enter. We followed his truck and Al's auto back the lane for nearly a mile going through pasture land and past a grove of trees. Topping a small rise we looked down to our left at a large house with a smaller building nearby. There were other out-buildings farther away. The large house was thought to have been built around 1840 with existing small buildings being added as "wings" over the years. Pillars, requisite of the period, stood at the front of the house. The owner was not living in the house but was having it extensively restored.

However, our reason for being there was to see the nearby structure: the house Robert Sharp Jr. built in 1794. Also, to get a sense of this very land his father purchased in 1761.

Tobacco was the main crop in 1700's Virginia and because of its rapid depletion of the soil's fertility new land was needed to continue planting the crop. This probably was the primary impetus for Robert Sharp Sr. moving from Henrico County to Albemarle. This land that had grown tobacco over two hundred years ago was now pasture. It was being used for the grazing of cattle. We went to the area where the limestone quarry had existed. It was near a small stream (Limestone Creek) near the highway. Robert Sharp Sr. sold this small acreage, quarry and kiln to Thomas Jefferson in 1771. The mortar produced was used in the building of Monticello and the University of Virginia in Charlottesville. Monticello was a few miles away from where we were standing.

Robert Sharp Sr., if nothing else, was an acquirer of land. Adjoining his original purchase was 400 acres for which the patent had not been completed. With Jefferson as his lawyer, Sharp successfully sued to gain ownership of the land. Jefferson's personal notes indicate that there were many interactions between the Sharps and he. Farm produce and livestock were provided to Monticello. Undoubtedly, the Sharps used the important skills of the blacksmith that resided at Monticello.

We were impressed with the Robert Sharp Jr. house. It was a 20 by 30 feet structure in excellent shape with a brick lower level and frame upper story. It had two levels with added space in an area topped by the peak of the roof. The building was being used as a storage shed with the clutter inside difficult to navigate for a room by room viewing.

On the exterior of the house one could see where a chimney had been removed, where doors had become windows, and new doors added later in the house's life. It was remarkably sturdy with brickwork that appeared original.

Robert Sharp died in 1808 and Robert Sharp Jr. died a few months later. The heirs sold the land and house in 1818 to James Monroe, the fifth President of the United States. The house was used as a law office.

Most of the Sharp heirs had scattered to the west, to the territories that had become the states of Indiana, Kentucky, and Ohio. It was there that lands were made available to Virginians who had served in the Revolutionary War. Robert Sharp Jr. acquired several land warrants in Ohio.

Robert Sharp Jr.'s House

The Limestone Farm is registered as a National Historical Site. The Jefferson and Monroe connections to the land, the Sharp house, and the historical Three Chopt Road that ran through the land were all pertinent factors in gaining such a distinction. Three Chopt Road, so named because it was marked by three axe marks on trees, was the land route between Richmond and the Blue Ridge Mountains. The indentation left by the wagons of long ago is clearly visible in the farm's soil today, close-by to the limestone quarry site.

Our visit ended at noon. It was a few hours well-spent. Al Sharp was very informative. Although our common ancestor is about seven generations back he has done much research in my line centered around the Limestone Farm.

Looking at Robert Sharp, Jr.'s house, the fields, the kiln site, the stream, the traces of the old road to Richmond, I felt connected. Was it because I wanted to be, or was it something deeper?

Epilogue: A year ago I wrote about my search for Henry Sharp's parentage. The essay appears earlier in this book. Several months after our visit to Limestone Farm, Al Sharp sent me a copy of the farm's sale to President James Monroe. The sellers, Robert Sharp, Jr.'s children, signed the sale document as well as the President. One of the children was my Henry Sharp. Bingo! Later I learned that the heirs had sold two of Robert Sharp, Jr.'s land patents in Ohio. When in Ohio, I researched these documents and saw Henry Sharp's name on both along with his living siblings. Henry was a township justice of peace in Ross County and he served as his siblings' representative in the land sales. One property was in Pickaway County and one was in Madison County. It was ample proof that I had reason for feeling "connected" when we visited Limestone Farm on Memorial Weekend. I had found Henry Sharp's "daddy."

December 2007

Resources:

National Park Service, National Register of Historical Places, VDHR File 002-0090, *Limestone Plantation*

National Park Service, National Register of Historical Places, VDHR File 44AB488, *Jefferson's Limestone Kiln*

TO OL' VIRGINNY

Part Two

It was our intent to leave right from the Limestone Farm to meet my cousins. I had been in contact with Louise Wade on Rockfish Valley Highway between Afton and Nellysford. I had told Louise that I would call when leaving Charlottesville. When I called, she said, "They are all waiting lunch for you at the farm." "Waiting lunch" and "all" caught my attention! Hurriedly, I told Louise to have them not wait, since we were nearly an hour away.

Looking at Marynelle, I said, "I'm not sure what I caused, but we are going to a farm, and it sounds like a lot of people are there and waiting lunch. All I had said is that we would like to stop by." Wasting no time we headed west toward the Blue Ridge Mountains. Finding Rockfish Valley Highway, we took it south running parallel to the Blue Ridge until we came to Louise's house. She answered the door with one foot in a shoe and one in a slipper. She pointed down saying she had just performed some "bathroom surgery on her foot." I immediately liked her and her humor.

The cousins were all descendants of the Rittenhouse clan, as was I. I had sometimes heard my Grandmother Sharp talk of her trip from Ohio to Virginia to see relatives. My father accompanied her at least once because he, too, spoke of the experience. I remember him telling me of visiting with Uncle Jud, a Confederate war veteran who had lost a leg in the conflict.

Louise turned down my offer to drive; rather she wanted us to follow her. We continued several miles, still in a southerly direction. I have always been taken with the Blue Ridge Mountains and their beauty. Now, here we were deep in their embrace soaking up the sights, while trying not to lose Louise. Finally, she turned into a lane at the end of which stood an impressive red-brick home with many out-buildings. They sat in a pocket of essentially level farm land snuggled between mountains to the west and hills to the east.

We met four granddaughters and one great granddaughter of Judson

Rittenhouse. The home we were in had been his, the granddaughters had been raised in the home, their mother, Sallie Mae, had been Judson's daughter. The great-granddaughter Mary Mathews Hoffman and her husband Walter now lived on the farm.

What a wonderful experience it was to meet them all. They were: Louise Wade who led us to the farm, Patsy Higginbotham who lived nearby at Afton, Sallie Elizabeth Lybarger from Staunton and Dorothy Revercomb who lived across the mountains near Deerfield in Augusta County. All were widows. Sister-in-law Hazel Phillips from nearby Nellysford was there as well. It was Hazel that had answered my internet query, the impetus for my wanting to come here.

There were photos taken, stories told and some remembered my grandmother and aunt visiting long ago. We toured the farm and house. On at least two occasions one would say, when looking at me, "He looks like a Rittenhouse!" Marynelle told me later that my reaction was always a little grin.

Dorothy told me of a memoir their Uncle Emmet had written about life growing up on the farm. She asked if I might like it. I jumped at the chance. I wanted to learn more about them and what life was like in the late 1800s in Virginia. But, also, I was hoping there would be some clue as to why Judson and his sister, my great-grandmother, went separate ways at the time of the Civil War.

Dorothy and Sallie both mentioned how happy "Mama" would be to know we met. I, too, had thoughts of my grandmother and father and how pleased they would be that we had traveled to Virginia.

It was a wonderful afternoon. That evening we headed up the road, again following Louise. This time she turned into an Italian restaurant near her home. The restaurant was owned by her daughter and son-in-law. We ate dinner, talked some more and finally parted.

It had been an extraordinary day. As we drove back toward Charlottesville, Marynelle turned to me, patted my leg and said, "You look like a Rittenhouse!"

Epilogue: Dorothy Revercomb did send me her Uncle Emmet's memoirs. It is chock full of folklore, poetry, character descriptions, and wonderful depictions of farm life as a boy. It was a stack of four hundred pages, a veritable goldmine for a history and genealogy enthusiast.

Judson's experience in the war and his refusal to take whiskey when his leg was amputated was told. There was no home for Judson to return to so his Uncle David took him in. Near the end of the four hundred pages was an answer to a question that I had long asked, but no relative could ever answer.

My great-grandmother Jane M. Rittenhouse left Albemarle County, Virginia, about the time of the Civil War and went to Ohio. I often wondered why. She was about twenty-one. Did she travel with others, was some relative awaiting her? I knew that she married in Ohio and to a former Confederate soldier from Rockbridge County in Virginia. What could two Virginians be doing in Ohio right after such a terrible, divisive conflict? Had they known each other in Virginia or did they meet in Ohio?

Uncle Emmet's memoirs provided some answers. An aunt that had previously migrated to Ohio in the 1840's returned to Virginia for a visit. Jane went with her to Ohio to see Rittenhouse relatives who had migrated there. The war started soon after preventing Jane from returning to Albemarle County. In her absence from Albemarle there were changes in her Virginia family. Her father died. Her stepmother no longer was a part of the family scene. Judson had gone to war, was wounded, and recovering at his Uncle David's. There was no family home awaiting Jane's return.

Jane married Alfred Robinson, a Confederate veteran, in 1869 and lived on a farm in Delaware County, Ohio. It was forty years before she saw her brother Judson again. They exchanged visits sometime after 1900.

January 2008

AFTERWORD

Writing has been an adventure. I have met and learned much from so many people; both published writers and those that have no intention of ever publishing anything. Lincoln has many good resources for a writer.

A few of the essays were passed among friends and relatives. Primarily, this was to check facts. In doing so papers came into the hands of a few unintended readers. Calls and emails were received from several. This became a source of encouragement to keep going and not quit. The essay *Ollie's Store* generated comments from some that had frequented the store about the time I had. I enjoyed reading of their experiences and memories of Ollie. *The Year I Turned Pro* elicited comments as well. Basketball was such a big part of our youth. It was good to hear from those I went to school with sixty years ago.

Hopefully, the genealogy-related writings will be of interest to those who like that sort of research. It was fun writing about *The Marryin' Squire*, the Sharps, and meeting those who have Rittenhouses (as I do) in the family tree. Seeing Thomas Jefferson's notes that referred to my Sharps was akin to hitting pay dirt for a genealogist.

Outsource It!! is an expression of my frustration with this phenomena that permeates our lives. It is seen as a panacea by industry and government for farming out tasks too difficult or costly to perform internally. Problems surface when those responsible write ineffective contracts for services and don't assure execution of those services. It is much easier to outsource for a widget that can be measured for quality than outsource for a service. Okay, I'll put aside the soapbox.

I hope old Laser Eye is available for a little tennis after lunch.

ADDENDUM

THE FAMILIES

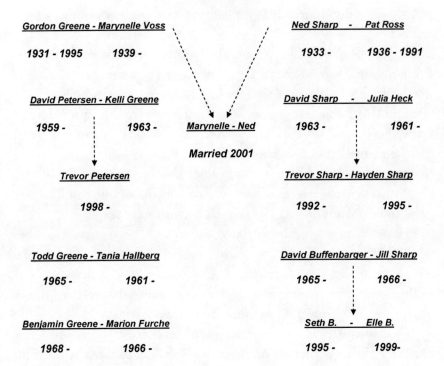

Gordon Greene - Marynelle Voss

1931 - 1995   *1939 -*

Ned Sharp - Pat Ross

1933 -   *1936 - 1991*

David Petersen - Kelli Greene

1959 -   *1963 -*

Marynelle - Ned

Married 2001

David Sharp - Julia Heck

1963 -   *1961 -*

Trevor Petersen

1998 -

Trevor Sharp - Hayden Sharp

1992 -   *1995 -*

Todd Greene - Tania Hallberg

1965 -   *1961 -*

David Buffenbarger - Jill Sharp

1965 -   *1966 -*

Benjamin Greene - Marion Furche

1968 -   *1966 -*

Seth B. - Elle B.

1995 -   *1999-*

ACKNOWLEDGEMENTS

A book was not in the plans when I first began to write. The essays began to accumulate over the years resulting in the question, "What do you plan to do with them?" Marynelle suggested binding them into a folder for family Christmas presents. Christmas passed and the folder idea grew into a book. Pulling that off has proved a bit more involved than I had expected, but Marynelle's encouragement, suggestions, and patience have been key to my staying with it. I owe a very big thanks to her.

Thanks are due to:

My "Shelton" cousins Ann Fletcher, Judy Bitner, and Dean Shelton. They managed to keep me "factually" on target via phone calls. Bill Shelton, who passed away in 2005, provided anecdotes of his Granddad Claude, which added much to the story telling;

Doug Tron, James Boblenz, and Dale Moury. These friends for over 65 years provided the names and events that had escaped me. There are several stories that would have been lacking significantly if not for their impressive recall;

My daughter, Jill Buffenbarger and daughter-in-law, Julia Sharp. They shared family stories of their children which caused the three of us to share laughs;

My son, David Sharp, who suggested some writing topics and happens to live under the same roof with *The Pathfinder;*

The University of Nebraska SAGE and OLLI writing classes led by Gordon Culver, Clarice Orr, and Marlene Johnson. These leaders, as well as the class members, helped improve multiple drafts;

Al Sharp who was invaluable in uncovering Sharp genealogy in colonial Virginia;

Lyle Vannier, Joyce Vannier, and John Keller. They volunteered to read the manuscript much to my benefit;

Jeanne Kern. Jeanne was an enormous help in many aspects of writing this book. Her recommendations were followed faithfully. Her willingness to help provided much comfort.

Any errors found in the book must be charged to me.

INDEX

Note: Page numbers in *italic* refer to pictures.

LaVergne, TN USA
22 October 2009
161688LV00003B/5/P